Becoming an Outstanding Geography Teacher

Becoming an Outstanding Geography Teacher supports all geography teachers in offering a wide range of approaches to teaching and learning that will stimulate and engage students.

Providing a variety of techniques for planning inspiring geography lessons, the book shows teachers how they can use current resources in a more innovative way to produce outstanding results. Chapters include sample lesson plans which demonstrate each technique with a step-by-step discussion of the development of the lessons, and have a strong focus on activating learning and supporting students on their individual learning journeys. The book covers all aspects of geography teaching, including:

- designing programmes of study
- differentiation
- questioning
- literacy and numeracy
- teaching A Level
- enquiry geography
- feedback and assessment.

Packed full of strategies and activities that are easy to implement, *Becoming an Outstanding Geography Teacher* is essential reading for newly qualified and experienced geography teachers who want to ensure outstanding teaching and learning in their classrooms.

Mark Harris has been a practising secondary school teacher for 15 years and now leads Teaching and Learning at his school. He is a Specialist Leader in Education in the Birmingham region. Mark designs and delivers professional development for schools in this area, and is also a Guest Lecturer in the School of Education at the University of Birmingham, UK.

Becoming an Outstanding Teacher

Series Editor: Jayne Bartlett

Becoming an Outstanding Languages Teacher
Steve Smith

Becoming an Outstanding English Teacher
Kate Sida-Nicholls

Becoming an Outstanding Mathematics Teacher
Jayne Bartlett

Becoming an Outstanding Geography Teacher
Mark Harris

For a full list of titles see: www.routledge.com/Becoming-an-Outstanding-Teacher/book-series/BARTLETT

Becoming an Outstanding Geography Teacher

Mark Harris

Routledge
Taylor & Francis Group

LONDON AND NEW YORK

First published 2018
by Routledge
2 Park Square, Milton Park, Abingdon, Oxon OX14 4RN

and by Routledge
711 Third Avenue, New York, NY 10017

Routledge is an imprint of the Taylor & Francis Group, an informa business

British Library Cataloguing-in-Publication Data
A catalogue record for this book is available from the British Library

Library of Congress Cataloging-in-Publication Data
A catalog record for this book has been requested

ISBN: 978-1-138-69718-8 (hbk)
ISBN: 978-1-138-69721-8 (pbk)
ISBN: 978-1-315-52237-1 (ebk)

Typeset in Melior
by Apex CoVantage, LLC
Printed and bound by CPI Group (UK) Ltd, Croydon, CR0 4YY

To my girls
Rosie, Florence and Martha

Contents

Contents

Illustrations

Figures

Illustrations

Tables

Illustrations

Acknowledgements

I would like to thank my mum and dad for their continued support and love, my wonderful girls for their joyous smiles and of whom I am extremely proud, and my wife Esther for her patience and understanding when I was working. Thank you.

CHAPTER 1

An introduction to outstanding teaching

Outstanding teaching is something that has been much written about over the years. Just as the educational discussion and dialogue have morphed and changed, so too has the term evolved. Once 'outstanding' was a definable set of criteria that could be ticked off and measured, but more recently it seems to have become an intangible term, misinterpreted and exploited. Regardless of the term's connotations, it is the pursuit of excellence that is the endeavour. Outstanding teaching is simply teaching that stands out, teaching that is 'inspirational', 'inspiring' 'challenging', 'consistent' and all those other terms used to describe what teachers feel outstanding teaching is all about.

The premise of this chapter is not to create a tick list of what to include in a lesson to make it outstanding, but rather that if you employ the features within this book on a regular and consistent basis you will develop a degree of automaticity. The habits you will have developed will result in your lessons becoming outstanding; the process you follow will lead to excellence. As you practise these techniques and strategies, whilst also strengthening your own already developed skill set, then you will begin to operate at a higher level, at a level that sees your students excel. As with many things, the success of these habits and strategies will depend on you. It is through practice that these strategies can develop into habits, and once you have instilled outstanding habits you are more than half-way there. This point cannot be emphasised enough: you must keep practising and never stop learning. 'Outstanding' is a mindset: if you have decided to be outstanding you must be prepared to work at it, because it is the result of hard work and consistent application of the strategies you have learnt. Practice is key.

What does 'outstanding' look like?

As we have already identified, 'outstanding' means different things to different people. However, following is a list of features I feel are necessary if a lesson is to be considered 'outstanding'.

For students, 'outstanding' is achieved when:

1   Students are actively engaged. This may be demonstrated by students asking considered geographical questions, willingly participating in questioning, offering answers and making relevant comments.

2   Students take ownership of their learning: the students make decisions on which challenges or questions they wish to complete and how they will go about discovering and answering them. These challenges can be within and outside of the classroom, and both are met with the same degree of engagement and enthusiasm.

3   Students take ownership of the assessment process: they are directly involved in the assessment process by reviewing what they have learnt, acknowledging what they need to do to improve and then acting on those targets. This is also achieved by their involvement in the development of the success criteria for assessments.

4   Students are able to learn, consolidate and then apply their skills, knowledge and understanding in a variety of settings, including extended writing, presentation and through oracy.

5   Students can learn effectively through an enquiry process. They are able to develop questions, recognise opportunities to discover and then explore their own learning, in order to solve problems and further their understanding.

6   Students demonstrate a growth mindset. They show tenacity and resilience when faced with challenges, and see setbacks and failure as learning opportunities.

For teachers, 'outstanding' is achieved when:

1   Geographical thinking is promoted at every opportunity. Students are encouraged to think like a geographer. They are challenged to make connections, link ideas and ask questions to further their knowledge and understanding.

2   Geographical skills are developed pragmatically.

3   Students are encouraged and supported to work independently to develop their skill set and conceptual understanding.

4   The teacher's enthusiasm and subject knowledge is shared with the class. This engages and inspires the students to greater achievements.

5   All students are appropriately challenged to work to the best of their ability.

6   Marking and assessment is used by the teacher to identify gaps in learning. This assessment process is then used to plan the next steps for the students, and offer support so that all students can make progress.

7   Planning is used to map the students' learning to give every possible opportunity for the students to make the best possible progress.

8   Questioning is used astutely and with skill to further students' understanding and assess progress.

In addition to those characteristics, there are a number of habits that outstanding teachers follow. It is important to recognise that outstanding teachers, whilst being proficient in many of these habits/skills, will not necessarily be outstanding in all areas. In fact they may excel in only a handful of skills, yet be considered outstanding because they optimise their 'best' skills and work to develop those skills they may consider to be less defined. To become outstanding it is important not to neglect those skills you already possess. In fact, it is vital that you develop and practise those skills to enhance them even more, as this is how you become an outstanding practitioner, not only learning new skills but also refining those skills that you consider to be your greatest assets.

I am sure that you will have your own thoughts and ideas on what you think constitutes 'outstanding'. Please note that here I do not talk about an 'outstanding lesson'. It's important to realise that not every lesson you teach will be outstanding, and there is nothing wrong with this. In fact we often learn more from our failures than from our successes. I see a lot of teachers teaching: some teachers can 'turn it on' and produce a wonderful all-singing and all-dancing, outstanding lesson, and yet for the remainder of the year they produce a lacklustre teaching performance. Then I can watch a teacher who, no matter which lesson you turn up to, will produce some consistently wonderful teaching. It may not always be 'outstanding', yet the diet of well-planned and delivered teaching shows clear progress over time, resulting in excellent exam results year after year. I know what I prefer to see. Consistency is key to an outstanding performance from both you and your students.

The good news is that you already possess everything you need to be outstanding: it is all within you. You must develop your mindset to achieve your ambitions. This can be both liberating and scary, but in reality 'outstanding' is a state of mind. You may not be outstanding yet because you haven't decided to be. Once you make the decision to be 'outstanding', commit to it, go to the edge of your comfort zone and see what you can achieve. Figure 1.1 outlines some key areas to focus on to become 'outstanding'.

As with the students you teach, you cannot get better without constructive feedback, and therefore it will be necessary to ask others to watch you teach to give you some ideas of what you could do to improve. I appreciate that this is never comfortable, yet it is a necessary step if you are to improve your performance and ergo the performance of your students. Seek assistance from your peers and your management team, and even ask for feedback from the students – which can often be truly insightful. Work on this feedback and then ask for a review of your performance after a few weeks. Regardless of the training/coaching programme that operates at your school, the best approach is for you to take ownership of your own development. Become your own coach and train yourself to peak performance.

Ask yourself the following questions:

- What do outstanding teachers do?
- What do they do differently from you?
- What's holding you back?

Outstanding teaching in a nutshell

- Outstanding teaching is a mindset.
- To become an outstanding teacher, develop outstanding habits.
- Practise makes progress: keep practising the strategies and techniques until you can operate with automaticity.
- It takes time to develop new habits. Small incremental improvements happen over time, so stick with it!

Figure 1.1 Outstanding teaching in a nutshell

Designing and developing a sequence of lessons

When you are first designing a series of lessons or scheme of work, one of the best approaches is to begin with the end in mind. Have a clear vision of which skills you want the students to have developed and what knowledge and understanding they need to acquire to allow them to be successful, both in their assessments and also for the next stage in their learning. The content and skills you are developing may be linked to a specific qualification, specification or to a national curriculum, thus this will often dictate exactly what you need to teach your students. It is therefore important to look at the bigger picture: how your lesson will fit into the scheme of work, then how that fits into the yearly plan and the key stage, and then how the key stage fits into the long-term plan for the students. You need to consider what geography education you are going to provide from the students' first day in the school to their last. When designing a key stage programme of study I consider how it will all fit together (see Figure 2.1, which shows the links between a single lesson to the school career of the students' you teach). What content and skills will I want to embed and foster to make the transition from one key stage to the next as smooth as possible?

Begin with the end in mind

At first sight it may appear that my only aim is to get the students to pass their exams, yet this is far from the case. I want to enthuse and impassion my students, creating a love of geography that will stay with them all their lives. I want to deliver fun, exciting and enjoyable lessons that will remain with them always, so that in future years students can look back and still recall that some of their favourite memories of school were in my classroom. Within this desire to create zealous geographers is my overriding aim of making sure that students achieve the best score/grade possible, so that they can go on to achieve whatever it is they wish to do or pursue any career they want to embark on.

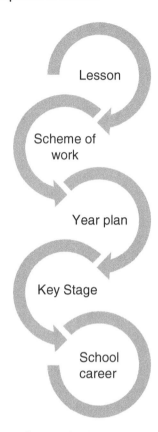

Figure 2.1 Connection from lesson plan to school career

The reality is that those aims will not just happen by luck; they need to be worked at and planned for. Therefore if I am going to succeed in developing high-achieving and enthusiastic geographers I need to begin with the end I have in mind, and I first need to consider the skills, knowledge and understanding that my students require in order to be successful in geography.

Geographical skills

The skills we are trying to develop are not just useful for the geography classroom but should be the necessary skills for 21st century learners to excel at university, the work place and in general life. To begin with, consider which skills your students need to be successful in their exams. I have listed what I consider to be the necessary skills students need to possess in order to become competent geographers, and these can be developed through their years at the school.

Geographical skills that are required to create successful students include the following.

Students should be able to:

- Make decisions based on different sources of evidence
- Use specialist geographical vocabulary
- Read and use a variety of maps, plans and atlases
- Use Geographical Information Systems (GIS) with confidence
- Interpret photographs, diagrams, data, newspapers, journals and information from the Internet
- Accurately analyse and interpret data, graphs, tables and charts
- Link ideas and concepts together
- Write appropriately for a range of audiences
- Use a range of numeracy and graphicity skills including the production, interpretation and analysis of line, bar, scatter and triangulation graphs, pie charts, chloropleth, isoline and dot maps
- Present to peers and a range of audiences with confidence
- Communicate with others using a range of technologies
- Contribute to collaborative projects
- Talk, read and write like a geographer
- Use fieldwork to create and test hypotheses, collect and present data that can be analysed and interpreted to draw conclusions, evaluate their own process and offer further research opportunities

Students should have:

- A detailed and accurate knowledge of case studies to support a wide variety of geographical contexts
- A range of exam techniques that allows the students to access the exam question
- An understanding of command words and question formula
- A conceptual understanding of the topic that allows them to apply their knowledge to questions
- Knowledge of place at a variety of scales, including continents, oceans, countries, regions and significant physical and human features
- An understanding of and an ability to apply the knowledge of processes and patterns

- An understanding of how human and physical geographies interact (syn-opticity)
- Research skills using multiple sources of information
- Literacy skills to be able to write descriptively and analytically, discursive writing

This list is by no means comprehensive, nor is it set in stone. Geography is such a dynamic subject; the nature of the skills may evolve and change through time.

Content: knowledge and understanding

Having identified the skills necessary for your students to be successful, it is then worth considering what content you need to cover with them. This represents the knowledge and understanding part of the planning Venn diagram (see Figure 2.2). When planning my Key Stage 3 programme I first look at which content they need to know at General Certificate of Secondary Education (GCSE) level, and I will try to link some of these topics together, whilst also bearing in mind that I want to offer breadth of knowledge rather than a diet of the same topics year after year. Therefore, I may well select certain topics in order to develop the students' knowledge throughout the key stages, whilst also offering other topics that the students want to study. Involving the students in the decision making process can yield a number of positives for the department: ask the students what they would like to study prior to organising your curriculum.

When I first started designing the key stages' schemes of work I created a topic list with a short blurb about each topic, and then I asked the students which topics they would like to study, having told them that certain topics would have to be covered. Each topic lasts for approximately a half term, therefore for about six weeks. This is just a system that works for the department at my school and you may be in a different position regarding the number of lessons or the organisation of geography. Nonetheless, involving the students in the decision making process can only serve to increase the engagement and enthusiasm for the subject.

Once you have created your list of topics to study, you can start to map out how the topics will fit together over the year and also over the key stages. Do you want the same topics to be repeated in each key stage? Do you want to teach a theme and merge topics together? Do you want the topics to be independent of each other and stand alone as separate topics? There is no comprehensive right and wrong answer to these questions, as we are all in different situations within our school. However, I would strongly urge you to think carefully at

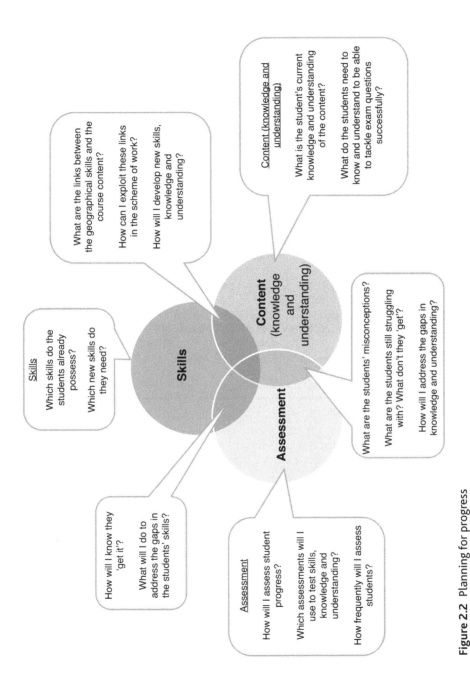

Skills

Which skills do the students already possess?

Which new skills do they need?

Content (knowledge and understanding)

What is the student's current knowledge and understanding of the content?

What do the students need to know and understand to be able to tackle exam questions successfully?

What are the links between the geographical skills and the course content?

How can I exploit these links in the scheme of work?

How will I develop new skills, knowledge and understanding?

What are the students' misconceptions? What are the students still struggling with? What don't they 'get'?

How will I address the gaps in knowledge and understanding?

How will I know they 'get it'?

What will I do to address the gaps in the students' skills?

Assessment

How will I assess student progress?

Which assessments will I use to test skills, knowledge and understanding?

How frequently will I assess students?

Figure 2.2 Planning for progress

this stage: how will your topics fit together to give your students the best experience you can give them within geography?

Table 2.1 presents an example of how a programme of study may look. This is based on a three-year Key Stage 3; however, I am aware that many schools now start to teach the GCSE course in Year 9. In this example the GCSE course does not start until Year 10, yet there is obviously some overlap of the topic which provides a base from which to work. In reality the Year 9 topics are from the GCSE specification, so students become immersed in the content in Year 9.

Table 2.1 Programme of study

	Autumn Term		Spring Term		Summer Term	
Year 7	Fantastic places	Maps	Risky world	India	China	Geography of the UK (fieldwork)
Year 8	Africa	Flooding (fieldwork)	Brazil	Russia	Coasts	Weather and climate
Year 9	Climate change	Ecosystems: rainforests	Population	Energy	Desert environments	Local fieldwork
Year 10	Hazards: tectonics	Hazards: tropical storms	Urban issues: global perspective	Urban issues: UK perspective	UK physical landscapes: rivers	Fieldwork
Year 11	Resources management: energy	UK physical landscapes: coasts	Ecosystems	Revision: pre-released material/topics		

Based on the AQA Geography specification

Table 2.1 shows the topics that have been selected after discussions with both staff and students. This is just a model that works for my school in our particular circumstance; you may well operate in a very different system. However you construct your schemes of work, you may consider teaching or using within your key stage planning the following list of geographical topics:

Physical geography

- Natural hazards: tectonic hazards and weather hazards
- Rivers
- Coasts
- Glaciation
- Biomes and ecosystems: rainforests, hot environments, cold environments
- Weather and climate including climate change

- UK landscapes
- Extreme environments
- Geology: rocks and scenery

Human geography

- Urban environments: urbanisation, changes to urban areas and sustainable settlements
- The development gap
- Food issues and management
- Energy issues and management
- Health issues and management
- Changing economies (national and international)
- Country profiles: including High Income Countries, Low Income Countries and Newly Emerging Economies, including India, Russia, China, Brazil, Kenya
- Fantastic places
- Industry: farming, manufacturing and tourism
- Transport
- Resources and the environment
- Settlements
- Population

Once we have the list of skills and content we want to cover, we can then start to map a programme of study around these key themes. The reality is that for students to be successful at GCSE work doesn't begin in the last few months of revision in Year 11, or even at the start of Year 10 – it begins on day one in Year 7. Every lesson counts. Therefore the programme of study that we design must aim to meet that final goal. What is it that we are doing in each lesson or topic that will help to contribute to the students being successful at GCSE? How will the lesson we deliver in the first week of Year 7 help to make the students be successful in their GCSE five years later?

As mentioned previously, when we are planning we need to begin with the end in mind. Thus when we are planning a sequence of lessons for a topic we need to follow the same format. Whether it is a National

Curriculum or an examination specification, I begin by asking myself the same two questions:

1   What is it that the students need to know by the end of this topic?

2   Which skills, knowledge and understanding can be developed within the year?

This forms the spine of my lessons, and I then continually refer back to this to make sure that I am on track: this allows me to strip out any content that does not fit a purpose. Figure 2.2 is a useful reference to support you to plan for progress, asking you to consider the key aspects of skills, content and assessment.

Exemplar: tropical storms

For the purpose of an example I will use the topic of tropical storms, a topic that features in many GCSE and A Level specifications.

What is the key content that the students need to know for their exam? Students need to know:

1   How the atmospheric circulation system works

2   The distribution of tropical storms

3   The features of tropical storms

4   The causes of tropical storms

5   The effects of tropical storms

6   The responses to tropical storms

7   The management and monitoring of tropical storms

8   A case study of a tropical storm event

I then consider how I can deliver each of these components within my lessons and offer an appropriate range of challenge, whilst also incorporating those skills identified earlier as being key to becoming a successful geographer.

I then link this to the assessment requirements of the course. How will I know that the students have understood and learnt the content? How will I assess this? Recent changes to the GCSE systems means that all GCSE courses now have to comply to certain assessment criteria.

As can be seen from Table 2.2, there is an increased emphasis on the application of knowledge. It is not good enough just to know a pattern or process; this then needs to be applied to a situation or scenario in order to adequately answer GCSE questions.

Table 2.2 Assessment criteria

Assessment Objective	Requirement	Weighting
AO1	Demonstrate knowledge of locations, places, processes, environments and different scales.	15%
AO2	Demonstrate geographical understanding of: • Concepts and how they are used in relation to places, environments and processes • The interrelationship between places, environments and processes	25%
AO3	Apply knowledge and understanding to interpret, analyse and evaluate geographical information and issues and to make judgements.	35% (10% applied to fieldwork context)
AO4	Select, adapt and use a variety of skills and techniques to investigate questions and issues and communicate findings.	25% (5% used to respond to fieldwork data and contexts)

(GCSE subject levels, conditions and requirements for geography: Ofqual, 2015).

Having considered my three strands – i.e. skills, content and the knowledge and understanding necessary to meet the assessment criteria – I then plan my lessons accordingly. Table 2.3 is an example of a planning matrix used to teach tropical storms.

Table 2.3 Example of a planning matrix for tropical storms

Specification content	Skills	Assessment
General atmospheric circulation model: pressure belts and surface winds	Using specialist geographical terminology	AO2
Global distribution of tropical storms (hurricanes, cyclones and typhoons).	Mapping; location of place.	AO1
An understanding of the relationship between tropical storms and general atmospheric circulation	Link ideas and concepts together	AO2
Causes of tropical storms and the sequence of their formation and development	Interpretation of photographs and diagrams	AO1
The structure and features of a tropical storm	Demonstrate an understanding of patterns and processes	AO1
How climate change might affect the distribution, frequency and intensity of tropical storms	Conceptual understanding that allows students to apply their knowledge (using previous knowledge to link to another issue)	AO2

(*Continued*)

Table 2.3 (Continued)

Specification content	Skills	Assessment
Primary and secondary effects of tropical storms	Use of case studies	AO3
Immediate and long-term responses to tropical storms	Decision making exercise	AO4
Use a named example of a tropical storm to show its effects and responses	Literacy skills: writing extended responses	AO3
How monitoring, prediction, protection and planning can reduce the effects of tropical storms	Research skills	AO4

Based on the AQA Geography specification.

The point of a planning matrix is to help you to see how the topic develops in terms of skills, knowledge and understanding, and the assessment levels. This then provides the framework for your lesson planning. Having a very clear view of what you need to teach and which skills you need to develop is a great starting point for all lesson planning. Figure 2.3 summarises the key aspects to planning a sequence of lessons.

Planning a sequence of lessons in a nutshell

- Begin with the end in mind.
- Identify the key skills that are required for your students to be successful at GCSE and A level.
- Develop these skills in every class you teach.
- Identify the key content students need to know to be successful at GCSE and A level.
- Teach this content throughout the key stages to develop their knowledge and understanding of the topic.
- Become confident with assessment criteria by using it within every topic that you teach.

Figure 2.3 Planning a sequence of lessons in a nutshell

Lesson planning
Minimal time, maximum impact

If we were to critically reflect on the lessons we teach, I would suggest that the majority of those lessons follow a similar pattern. This is because we have ingrained habits that we have developed over the years that create fixed routines and patterns to our teaching. Not that these habits are necessarily bad – it's just that if we are doing the same things we did year after year, lesson after lesson, I would question the progress we are making with our teaching. Are the habits that we have developed still in-line with our current aims? The habits we have developed are partly due to the planning process we have used in the past. In fact, I would suggest that our planning patterns have not changed that significantly from when we first joined the profession. It may be time to take a fresh look at our planning and see it there are possible ways to streamline the process to make planning more effective and efficient.

Jayne Bartlett recognises one of the key points to planning: 'When developing a lesson, think about how you are going to plan for learning rather than how you plan to teach' (Bartlett, 2014: 5). I used to make this mistake in my early career: my planning was centred on me, what would I say and what exciting resources would I make. There was little regard for the actual learning that would be taking place; it was focused on my teaching. I would produce some wonderful worksheets yet fail to consider if they were really challenging for the students, or if they already knew the content, or even if they could access the work. As soon as I changed my thinking from 'I' to 'them' my teaching drastically improved. How can I challenge them, how can I support them and how will I question them?

Planning 'outstanding lessons'

Stage 1: proper preparation prevents poor performance

It begins even before the students have entered the classroom. Have an effective seating plan. Consider carefully where your students will sit. I sincerely believe that a good seating plan can drastically reduce your behaviour management issues. I always speak to colleagues at the start of the year to discover what students work well together and which students need to be kept apart. Remember this is your classroom, so you decide where the students sit. If you feel it needs changing after a few weeks, then do so.

When you can, have the students' books on their desks before the lesson starts – this makes the start of the lesson slick so time is not wasted. It enables the students to engage with your starter activity with minimal disruption.

Meet and greet your students at the door. This is a great habit for several reasons.

- You can remind students of the class routines: 'come in, sit down, get on with the starter challenge on the board'.
- Having a pocket full of pens allows you to distribute pens at the door as the students come in rather than having students who need pens disrupt the learning later.
- A friendly smile or little joke can help to diffuse behaviour issues that certain students may exhibit before they even enter the class.

These three simple devices of a seating plan, books on desks, and meet and greet all help to create a culture of high-quality learning. They set defined boundaries and the students are clear that this classroom is an environment of high expectations.

Stage 2: starter

Students should expect to start work as soon as they enter the classroom. The starter activity should mean something to the students and go some way to support their learning. The challenge should aim to consolidate previous work and link to the current lesson. A range of starter activities are discussed in Chapter 4.

Stage 3: objectives – begin with the end in mind

The first thing to consider is what you want your students to know or be able to do by the end of the lesson. This should be linked to the scheme of work or the course specification. There is little point in making this objective too grand or all encompassing; the aim is to produce small incremental gains, allowing the students to master a certain aspect of the course before moving on. It is also worth remembering at this point that progress is not linear. Students will not progress at a uniform or proportional amount each lesson. In fact, in some lessons they may appear to make little progress whilst in others they may be making huge bounds in their knowledge and understanding.

Having considered what you want the students to know or be able to do by the end of the lesson, you also need to consider the following questions in tandem: What's the point? Why do they need to learn this? How does this relate to the big picture of what you teach? Are you able to justify to yourself and the students exactly why they are learning what you are about to teach them?

Whatever objective you set, make sure it is measurable. Students need to be able to demonstrate whether or not they have mastered the skills or demonstrate that they have understood the content. As the teacher you need to know how students are progressing, which students have mastered the skills and which students require support and time to fully grasp the concepts, ideas or skills. This will then inform your planning for the next lesson. Are there aspects of the lesson you need to go over again? How will you consolidate the learning that has occurred? Will students be given the opportunity to apply what they have learned? All these questions will need to be considered.

Following is a list of useful objective stems.

You may find it useful to use stems such as 'By the end of the lesson you will . . .'

- *Know that* . . . (knowledge and content-based information)
- *Understand how/why* . . . (understanding and comprehension of concepts, ideas and processes)
- *Develop/be able to* . . . (skill acquisition and understanding)
- *Develop/be aware of* . . . (values and attitudes, empathy, global citizenship, others' views, conflict of opinion)

An alternative is to phrase objectives in terms of the stem 'We are learning to . . . so that . . .'

Stage 4: learning question

Having defined your lesson objective, the learning question you pose aims to create curiosity and engage your students to the lesson. I feel that turning your objective into a learning question helps to 'hook' students as well as making it more accessible and interesting. For example, the objective 'To know that food production is a global process' can be changed into 'Why do my strawberries come from Egypt?' You may disagree, yet I feel this is a far more interesting title to investigate.

As well as making your lesson more interesting to the students, another major benefit is that a learning question acts as a bookend to the lesson. You begin the lesson with the learning question and then end the lesson by referring to the same question. Referring to the learning question during the plenary or 'strengthening session' allows you to evidence clear progress or inform you of misconceptions or gaps in the learning. A final activity may be to write a paragraph answering the learning question. This shows clear progress of your students and allows you to read their work to check their understanding, thus informing your next lesson. Did they all get it? If not, why not? What do I need to do next lesson to make sure they understand it?

Stage 5: success criteria

Success criteria are the maps that show students what they need to do in order to progress and achieve. They help students to focus on the learning outcome and provide autonomy so they can achieve their own goals. Success criteria should be aimed right at the top of students' ability and slightly outside of their comfort zone to really challenge and inspire them to create their very best work.

There are a few points to consider when writing success criteria:

- Be clear with yourself about what success looks like; in other words, know what you want from the students.
- Communicate this message clearly.
- Success criteria should increase the level of challenge for all students.
- Get students to discuss with you their understanding of the criteria. This minimises ambiguity and uncertainty, so that all students know exactly what is expected from them. To help you achieve this, write your criteria clearly in student-friendly language so that all students can access it.
- Show students what success looks like. A sample of model work can save valuable time, present a definitive example of what you want them to achieve and also show them what can be achieved by students in the same age group.
- Success criteria do not have to be constrained to one lesson or to one topic. If you really consider your criteria carefully, then they can be applied to several lessons throughout the year and therefore reduce your workload. For example, you may develop generic criteria for extended writing or map work that can used for different year groups and different topics.

- Success criteria are all about getting students to aim higher and improve their work, rather than complete a number of tasks. For this reason the criteria should focus on knowledge development, depth to understanding concepts or ideas or developing skills.

Stage 6: challenges

The challenges or activities for students to complete will often form the main body of the lesson. They should be designed to complement and support what you are hoping to achieve. The challenges should fit the learning objective rather than the learning objective fitting around the activities. Remember it is all about student progress. How will your challenges help to develop students' understanding or develop their skills? Linked to these challenges will be your use of success criteria, differentiation and evidence of progress.

Following are a number of questions to help you develop challenges aimed at improving student performance and enhancing their progress.

- How will your activity help to achieve the learning objective?
- How will it operate? If the activity involves group work, will this be based on ability or friendship groups? What are the logistics of the activity? How will you give out the equipment?
- How will you differentiate the challenge so it is appropriate for all students?
- How will you make sure they know what to do?
- How do you want the work to look in their books?
- How will you support low attaining students and how will you stretch the higher attaining?
- What high-order questions will you ask?
- What do you predict the answers to be? How will you resolve any misconceptions?
- How will the students demonstrate what they have learnt?
- How will you check their progress?
- Is there an opportunity to develop their literacy or numeracy skills?
- Is there an opportunity for students to consolidate or apply their learning?
- How will students know if they have been successful?
- What are the barriers to learning? What will stop this lesson from being successful?
- What can you do to solve those barriers?

Please note that I would not expect you to be writing an answer to each of these questions; they are simply there to stimulate thought. Also I would not necessarily expect your lesson to contain all of the points listed. It is not realistic to expect every lesson to be fully differentiated with opportunities to develop literacy and numeracy as well as both consolidate and apply all the learning within a lesson. But if you have thought about each question, this guarantees that you will not have missed a learning opportunity.

Empathise with the students when considering challenges. Are the activities you are planning interesting and enjoyable? Not every lesson can be, but try not to deliver the same type of lesson time and time again. Variety is the spice of life and you may find a new approach is all that is needed to reignite and create a spark in your students. Chunk activities if you find this works well to keep your students engaged and on task with the learning. Breaking up a large concept or idea makes it far more accessible for the students and they will generally participate more.

Whenever I introduce a challenge or activity I go through the same routine: I first ensure that all students are listening, then I break the challenge down into steps and I make sure that I don't overload them with too much information. If they need to know more, I can tell them the other stages once they have begun. Having given them the instructions, I then ask a student to repeat back to me what they have to do. I may then ask him/her to elaborate on the instruction. I will then ask another student the same thing. At this point I may ask a student who struggles to retain information or a student who I don't think was listening properly. This prevents them from asking me later or being off-task when the challenge begins. The quality of the instruction can help to minimise disruption.

Stage 7: questioning

Planning high-order questions is an outstanding habit to cultivate. High-order questions guarantee high-order thinking and responses, skills we are keen to develop with our students. Mapping out when and what questions you will be asking steers the lesson to excellence, creating increasing levels of challenge for all students and supporting an improvement in performance. Two or three high-order questions may be all that is necessary to create further curiosity or to challenge the students to think at a higher level. Chapter 5 on questioning will help you to develop and implement this vital skill of outstanding teaching.

Stage 8: plenary or 'strengthening bond' session

This is the stage where students may have the opportunity to demonstrate what they have learnt or to consolidate or apply their knowledge, understanding or skill. Do not underestimate the impact of a well-designed plenary. It

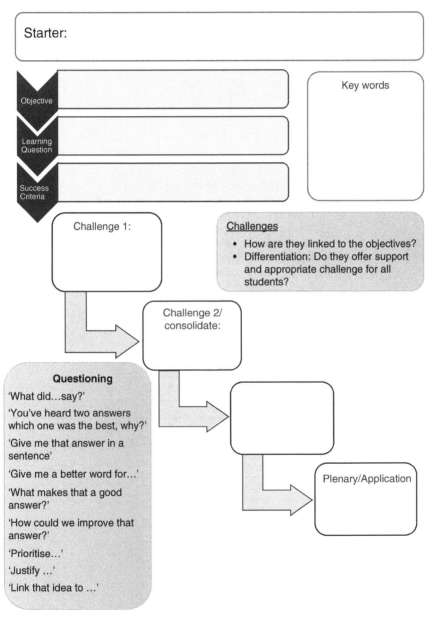

Figure 3.1 Lesson plan template

supports recall, helps to consolidate the learning that has taken place and can help to commit learning to long-term memory. It is important to set adequate time aside to complete this stage. Obviously this depends on the lesson and what the students have been learning, but this final session should not simply be more of the same or an ill-conceived 'add on' to the lesson. Chapter 15 on strengthening bonds contains a number of ideas to support your students to reach peak performance and to aid their progress. Figure 3.1 is a planning sheet that can be used to tie the stages of planning together, while Figure 3.2 highlights the key components of planning.

Planning in a nutshell

- Proper preparation prevents poor performance: get organised with seating plans, books on desks and the starter activity on the board.
- Have total clarity on what you want to achieve by the end of the lesson.
- Use learning questions to create curiosity and to engage the students.
- Design success criteria so both you and the students know what success looks like.
- Create challenges that are accessible and challenging for all. It doesn't matter if they do not get the skills, ideas or concepts the first time. Progress often involves failure, struggle and resilience.
- Plan your questions and predict the responses.
- Consider the barriers to the lesson being a success and then put in plans to mitigate against those barriers.
- Use plenaries to 'bookend' the lesson.

Figure 3.2 Planning in a nutshell

CHAPTER 4

Outstanding starters
How to start in the right way

As in life, first impressions count, so the first impression the students have of the lesson will help to set the benchmark. The importance of a good start to a lesson cannot be overestimated. An effective starter should be planned and you need to consider how it contributes to the students' learning journey. When you are considering your starter activity it is vital to ensure that it serves a clear purpose. What are you trying to achieve with the activity? Is it to clear up misconceptions from a previous lesson? Is it to demonstrate model work for the other students to learn from and aspire to achieve? Is it to motivate students to achieve more or to make connections between lessons? Whatever the answers are to these questions, the starter must fit into the bigger picture. In essence: give something meaningful.

Give something that means something

Outstanding starters have the following features:

- They have a clear purpose.
- They are linked to prior learning.
- They help students to link to new learning.
- They provide a challenge to students with minimal input from the teacher.
- They establish pace.
- There is a clear routine.

When asking the students to engage with a starter challenge, it may be worth considering how you will ensure that all students are engaged with the activity. I ask my students to write down their thinking. This makes the activity more rigorous, and also makes the students accountable as you can clearly see those students who have yet to put pen to paper. Consider the instruction that you give. Rarely do all thirty students turn up at once, thus if you are giving verbal instructions you will need to repeat them several times; better to have one clear instruction written on the board or to establish habits so that the students know exactly what to do when entering the classroom, therefore reducing disruption and off-task behaviour.

Starter challenges

Following are twelve starter challenges that I use on a regular basis with my classes. They have proved to be the most effective ways to engage and stimulate the class, linking learning together and proving the base to build the lesson on. As with all of the ideas, building up a clear routine and habit with the students ensures that the starters are swiftly incorporated into the lesson so the lesson starts with clear purpose.

Why is this so good?

For this challenge students are required to read and analyse a piece of work. This may be work from the prior lesson used to help students make connections between the last lesson and the current lesson. In essence the students become 'learning detectives', trying to unpick the answers and discover why the work got such a high grade or score. After students read the work you could ask them to either write on the board why it is so good or add sticky notes, or simply write in their exercise books. The aim is for the students to recognise the knowledge and skills demonstrated by a student who achieved a high grade or score and thus are able to improve their own understanding of what makes great work. In time, if you repeat this activity on a regular basis, students will understand the necessary content and skills required for success. For example, a piece of written work may show the following qualities that students are able to identify:

- Use of key terms
- Linked ideas
- Case study information or examples
- Impressive range of vocabulary
- Figures used to support the answer

If students have recorded this information in their books, then this can be referred to again when they undertake a similar piece or work, and thus they can become targets to improve their own work. When students have completed the work, I then ask them to highlight their answers to evidence where they have actioned their targets. It therefore becomes very clear to both students and teacher when targets have not been met, and ergo what students need to include to further improve their work.

What are they saying?

The challenge illustrated in Figure 4.1 requires students to think and consider carefully what the person may be saying about the scene in the picture. They must draw on their knowledge and understanding of a given situation or scenario to fill in the speech bubble. This of course will allow students to offer a wide range of answers, depending upon their understanding of the topic. Some students may offer a detailed explanation of the formation of tropical storms, along with a synopsis of the likely effects if the storms hit land. Other students may give a brief answer focusing on the amount of cloud cover. You may want to offer support by having a number of keywords on the board that students need to include in their answer, for example: eye wall, low pressure, anticlockwise. These provide the necessary support so that all students are able to access the question, rather than students not knowing what to do and therefore being off task.

Figure 4.1 What are they saying?

What are they thinking?

Although this activity is similar to 'What are they saying?' this question can generate a greater depth of thinking and application of prior knowledge. The activity can be used on a number of levels: at a basic level you may just want the students to respond with a verbal answer, saying what they consider the person/people to be thinking; at a higher level you may ask the students to come up with questions that they would like to ask the person/people in the photograph. Students could then write these questions in their exercise books or come to the front of the class and write their question around the picture on the board. These questions could be referred to throughout the lesson and used in the lesson plenary. You may want to ask a student to pretend to be a person in the photograph and hot seat him/her at the front of the class, with other students required to develop questions to ask.

For example, for the scene shown in Figure 4.2 students came up with the following questions:

'How big is your family?'

'Why is your family so big?'

'What job do you have?'

'Why did you move to the city?'

Figure 4.2 What are they thinking?

'Where do you get your water from?'

'Have you ever been really ill?'

'What is your life like?'

This activity allows you to gain an understanding of the group's current knowledge and thinking, whilst providing you with the opportunity to challenge misconceptions and ask further deeper questions to develop their understanding of the topic area.

Scrabble

This is a fantastic starter that can be used for multiple lessons and requires minimal preparation. Take a photograph of a selection of Scrabble letters and present this to the class. The challenge is then for the students to come up with as many words related to the topic as they can using the letters provided. You can add as many letters as you feel are necessary to match the age or ability of the class. As can be seen in the right-hand photograph in Figure 4.3, I have added more letters and a blank piece to support the class. You could even play the 'Countdown' theme tune to create tension and to make the activity time based. However you use this idea, it has the class captivated.

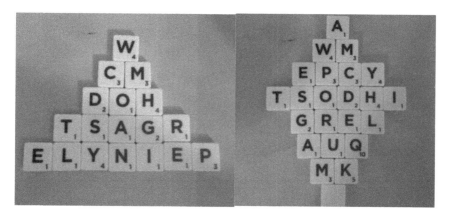

Figure 4.3 Scrabble

Ten questions

As far as ideas go, this is not a particularly imaginative one or an idea that will wow the education world. However, there are few other activities that I know of that get the class settled more quickly and are such a powerful learning device for both you and the student. Students are told that they have 3 minutes to revise before they start the quiz: this gives those latecomers to the class time to arrive and settle. Then simply ask the students to turn to the back of their books and ask them ten questions based upon prior learning. These need to be quick-response short answers so the activity does not stretch on too long, but the questions need to test the knowledge and understanding of the students. This does not require detailed preparation, merely some thought as to where you consider there may be any gaps in learning, and linking, where possible, to potential questions on future exams. This 5-minute review of prior learning helps to make connections and improve recall.

Following is an example of ten questions I used with a Year 10 class which had been studying tropical storms.

1 What is the temperature needed for tropical storms to form?
2 What is the name given to tropical storms that affect the coastline of Japan?
3 Name one Low Income Country affected by Hurricane Matthew.
4 Tropical storms are measured on which scale?
5 Give one reason why tropical storms die out.
6 In which region of the world do we find cyclones?
7 What must the wind speed be for storms to be considered to be 'tropical storms'?
8 Give one feature of a tropical storm.
9 Give the name of one town or city affected by Hurricane Katrina.
10 Name one way in which people can predict, protect or prepare for tropical storms.

Listen to the responses given – these can highlight misconceptions or gaps in the students' learning, which can then inform future planning. For example, if few of my students know that the sea temperature needed for tropical storms to form is 26°C, then it is clear that I need to revisit my 'What causes tropical storms?' lesson. It is worth remembering that you cannot simply look at the final scores to judge the merits of your teaching and their understanding. You need to investigate where the gaps in knowledge are. For example, two students may have both scored 7/10 yet be making mistakes in very different areas of the topic. You could carry out a quick 'hands up' poll to discover which questions the students got wrong. This may help to highlight the gaps in learning.

Six degrees of separation

This idea was developed by Frigyes Karinthy, who based the learning on the theory that we are all connected by at least five acquaintances. 'Six degrees of separation' is built on the notion that all living things – and everything else in the world – is six or fewer steps away from each other. Therefore, there is a chain of people or things that cause us all to be connected in some way.

For this to work as a starter, first select your topic or theme. Then you can use either pictures or simply write down the numbers 1 to 6 on the board, with your final destination written down next to number 6. Number 1 could be either a picture or a word, which the class then has to connect to item 6 in five steps or connections.

For example (see Figure 4.4):

1   Coffee is a cash crop.

2   Coffee companies are multinational companies operating around the world.

3   Coffee grows in tropical areas.

4   It's grown on plantations.

5   Trees have to be cleared for plantations.

6   . . . which results in DEFORESTATION.

Figure 4.4 Six degrees of separation

Model work

The use of model work to demonstrate what success looks like can be a hugely powerful tool in raising the expectations of the class, and also in demonstrating what excellent work involves. It can become part of your teaching repertoire. Few activities can help students to access what they are striving to achieve as well as this technique. I either scan or project a piece of work onto the board by using a visualiser; this is normally a piece of work from a previous lesson. Students are given time to reflect on and review what they did during the last lesson, and also to set personal targets for what they need to do to improve their work, whether this is the previous work or targets for the next time an extended answer is completed. The instruction for the class is 'Read the work and critique it.' To begin with, students may require prompts to help them to develop their critiquing skills. These could include:

- 'What makes this piece of work so good?'
- 'What has been included that means this work gets a high score?'
- 'Assess the key points of their written response.'
- 'Which part is your favourite, and why?'
- 'Prioritise the main points from the answer.'

Having asked the students to assess the work, I then highlight the key features with them. Following this I may ask the students to set themselves a target; this may be a target that they need to act on when they are writing their answer, or a target that they need to refer to in future lessons when they are writing an extended answer. The use of model work as a starter is both engaging and insightful for the students. They enjoy reading others' work and seeing what makes that work so good, as well as learning what they should be including to make their work better in the future.

Voice over

For this challenge I play a short excerpt of a video on a loop with the volume off. The students are then challenged to either describe the scene or to narrate the clip. If the clip involves dialogue between people you could ask several students to narrate the scene together, with each student acting as a different character.

Examples

Tropical rainforest: Find a clip of a tropical rainforest and ask the students to describe the scene. They may include such details as 'There are emergent trees which have grown so tall to reach the sunlight. Steam is rising off the trees due to the high daytime temperatures and the transpiration taking place.' The aim is for students to use a range of keywords to describe what they are watching. You could then play the clip again, with the original narrative, to see how closely the students' description matched the original.

Life in a squatter settlement: show a clip of a typical squatter settlement and ask the students to narrate the 'walk through'. What would they see, hear and smell? You may want to show a clip of an interview with a resident and ask the students to predict both the questions and the answers being given.

Picture this . . .

As the saying goes, 'a picture paints a thousand words', and for a geography teacher pictures also hold a thousand questions for students to think about. The advantage of using a picture is that it can be a stimulus for so much discussion and debate. This activity can be used as a starter, but can also develop into a main activity or even the majority of the lesson, depending on how you want the lesson to go and how it marries with the aims of your lesson.

Simply present a picture on the board and then ask the students to either individually or in pairs discuss what is happening in the picture. Ask them to jot down the first ideas in the back of their exercise books; you can later ask them to prioritise from the list the things they consider to be the most important. Use a range of question stems to help them with their thinking, such as:

- What links you to the picture?
- What do you think the scene looked like in the past?
- How will it look in the future?
- Can you offer any solutions to the problem/issue?
- What do you think is happening outside of the photograph?
- Where in the world do you think this is? Why?
- If you were there, what would you . . .
  - See?
  - Hear?
  - Smell?
  - Feel?

All these questions are intended to engage students and to challenge them to think more deeply about the issues or the scenario presented in the photograph. They demand that students contextualise the photograph and think at a higher level, especially when you ask them to give their 'best' thinking about the picture.

This activity can be developed further by using a questioning matrix that was first developed by John Sayers and later expanded by John Haines. It uses a number of question stimuli to get students to think more deeply. It is based on Socratic questioning, which has a six-step process:

1 Clarify

2 Challenge assumption

3 Evidence for argument

4 Viewpoints and perspectives

5 Implications and consequences

6 Question the question

Start by choosing a question stem from the vertical column shown in Figure 4.5 and then select a question from the horizontal column. For example: 'What will?' 'Who might?' 'How can?' Then challenge the students to answer the questions at a range of levels. In practice a question matrix could look like the example in Figure 4.6.

You could ask students to pick three question combinations from the matrix, then to write their answers on sticky notes and stick them in the relevant areas on the board.

Using Figure 4.6 as an example, the students created the following questions:

Who is involved in the flood?

How might the flood affect local people?

Why has the flood occurred?

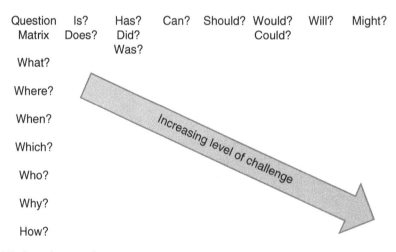

Figure 4.5 Question matrix

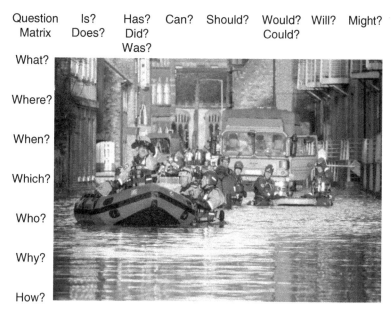

Question Matrix	Is? Does?	Has? Did? Was?	Can?	Should?	Would? Could?	Will?	Might?
What?							
Where?							
When?							
Which?							
Who?							
Why?							
How?							

Figure 4.6 Question matrix for flooding

Memory maps

Memory maps are a great way to get students to consider distances, scale, and location and relation of places and landmarks – all vital geographical skills necessary to be successful. This starter can be delivered in the following way: you may have a map projected onto the board with the instruction that students have 3 minutes to study the map and commit it to memory before they draw it themselves; you may give them an individual copy for them to study before telling the students to turn it over for their attempt at redrawing the map from memory, trying to recall as many features as possible. Students can then compare their map to those of their partners and peers and then look at the original map to compare and contrast their work.

A useful strategy to help support the students is for them to imagine the map is divided into four quarters and then to concentrate on one quarter at a time – if you choose to allow the students to look at the map four times. Support them by telling them that they need to be as accurate as possible, so ask which methods they could use to be successful. Usual responses include:

- Add the main features first.
- Think about the distances between landmarks.

This activity can be made more challenging by asking students to push their pencils through a piece of paper so that they are unable to see what they are drawing underneath. This level of challenge always excites the class and all students become more engaged with the task.

What if . . . ?

This idea is adapted from a Mike Gershon starter activity (www.mikegershon.com). Students are required to consider the outcomes and consequences of a particular event or scenario. This may be a statement, linked to a picture or a short video. It promotes deeper thinking and requires students to consciously evaluate a situation or circumstance. Students may be asked to respond verbally or in their exercise books, work as a pair, in groups or individually. The aim for this quick starter is to engage students and hook them with geographical thinking. I find that this activity meets both criteria wonderfully.

Examples

- **What if** we had another Ice Age?
- **What if** nobody was allowed to migrate?
- **What if** we could not trade with any other nations?
- **What if** we could eradicate malaria?
- **What if** a super volcano erupted?

Would you rather . . . ?

In a similar style to the starter 'What if . . . ?' you pose the question 'Would you rather . . . ?' to the class. This may be based on two conflicting ideas or concepts or similar solutions to the same problem. Student responses can be either verbal or written, and you may want individual answers or you may provide the opportunity for discussion through pair work.

Examples

- **Would you rather** be affected by an earthquake or a volcano?
- **Would you rather** migrate to the city but be separated from your family, or live with your family but in desperate poverty?
- **Would you rather** live in the Sahara Desert or in Antarctica?
- **Would you rather** live in the inner city or the suburbs?

Logistics of starters

As mentioned previously, the starter should require minimal instruction from the teacher so that all students are able to engage with the activity without the need for complex instructions or the provision of a plethora of resources. For that reason, the following three points will help your starter to achieve your aims:

1　Have the activity either on the board or on student desks ready for when they enter the classroom; students then have no excuse not to engage with the activity straight away. Make sure that the instructions that go with the challenge are accessible for all students.

2　Have the students' exercise books on their tables ready for them. Put them out before the first lesson, at break and lunchtimes and at the very end of the previous lesson whilst the class is packing away. This helps to support good classroom behaviour, so that students are not wandering around the classroom, nor are they idly chatting whilst waiting for their book to begin their work. It establishes purpose and ensures your lesson begins efficiently. Have paper on your desk and pens available ready to distribute as necessary for students to take if they have forgotten equipment. This reduces those barriers which may stand in the way of some students beginning the task.

3　Establish a routine: the key to successful starters is for the students to have developed the habit of engaging with them. This is just practice. You need to practice with them how to engage with your challenges and the students must come to know that when they enter the classroom there will be an activity on the board ready for them. Create your own routines so that the students get into the habit of sitting down and accessing the activity. Figure 4.7 summarises the key aspects to outstanding starters.

Starters in a nutshell
- Give something that means something.
- Be clear on the purpose of the starter: to demonstrate, consolidate, explore, reflect, evaluate, recall.
- Use starters to establish a routine to your teaching practice.
- Starters set the pace and tone of the lesson.
- Make your starters accessible for all with minimal input from you.

Figure 4.7 Starters in a nutshell

CHAPTER 5

Questioning

Questioning is at the heart of all outstanding teaching; in fact, questioning is what most 'outstanding' teachers spend most of their time doing. 'Outstanding' teachers ask a range of questions aimed at gauging the students' knowledge and understanding, questions to engage the students with the subject or topic, questions to develop deeper understanding, questions to clarify what is being taught and questions to assess if the students have got it. Have they made progress? 'Outstanding' teachers understand the power of a good questioning technique. In fact, I believe that questioning techniques are not something you can simply learn and become proficient in during a staff training session. These techniques take time to develop, through practice, mistakes, feedback, perseverance and self-analysis. Done well, questioning can help to unlock a student's potential. The questioning interaction that you have with a student can be the catalyst for something great; it may be the piece in the jigsaw that the student was missing, but through your questioning all the pieces finally fit and big picture is clear. Done badly, questioning can create confusion and misconception, and it can foster low self-esteem. Therefore questioning must be regarded as a key skill which teachers should strive to continually develop and improve.

The first key area that needs to be tackled is how to get all the students involved, which requires that you do not repeatedly call on the same handful of high-attaining students who have their hands up every time you ask a question. It is understandable why teachers do this. They are pretty much guaranteed a correct answer each time they ask a question and there is no conflict involved; this is much easier than trying to cajole an unwilling student to offer an answer, and the teacher doesn't need to repeat previously taught content, plus he/she will feel the students have been taught well enough for at least someone to know the answer to their questions. In fact, it appears a win-win situation all round. The teacher feels content that the lesson has been well taught, the high-attaining students are satisfied because they got the answers right and therefore they have increased their own self-worth, and the students who don't know the answer have managed to get through the lesson without being picked, which may have resulted in embarrassment and/or ridicule. Unfortunately, this technique hinders progress. There is a very high possibility that the students who had their hands up knew the answers before they entered the class, and those students who didn't answer are no nearer to knowing if they do truly understand what you have just taught them. In addition they have been denied the opportunity to express their thought or to ask further questions to develop their own understanding of the subject.

It may be worth considering why it is that students are reluctant to answer questions. You can do this by asking your class. Following are some points that I gleaned from discussions with students:

Why don't you like answering questions in class?

- I don't want to look a fool if I get it wrong.
- I don't like to talk in class.
- What if I get it wrong?
- I can't be bothered. . . . always answers anyway.
- I don't know the answer.
- Everyone else is cleverer than me.

You will notice that the majority of the students' responses are centred around self-esteem and appearing to be a failure if they are wrong. Few students spoke about questioning as an opportunity to learn more, or exhibited the 'growth mindset' necessary to develop. 'Growth mindset' is a term now widely used and accepted within education as a driver for success. The term was first coined by Carol Dweck in her book *Mindset: How you can fulfil your potential* (2012). It refers to the ability of some students to see challenges as opportunities to learn and grow (growth mindset), yet some students (with a 'fixed mindset') see challenges as insurmountable obstacles that they are never going to be able to overcome – so why should they bother trying? This is obviously a very brief snapshot of Dweck's excellent work, and I encourage you to read more on the topic as it can help to improve your classroom practice.

So if we recognise that students' reluctance to answer questions can partly be due to fear of failure, what can we do to reduce this fear?

Developing a growth mindset when questioning

Students, like us all, do not simply fall into one of the two camps: 'fixed' or 'growth' mindset. Rather, we can all show the two extremes, and all the parts in between, when faced with different challenges. When learning new teaching strategies I personally have a very open growth mindset, yet if I was asked to learn to play the piano I know I would struggle and exhibit a fixed mindset, saying things such as 'It's no good, I'll never learn' or 'This is pointless – I'm rubbish.' In reality, of course, I could learn if I was willing to dedicate my time and effort to it. Like us, students can display the full spectrum of attributes from fixed to growth mindsets.

Create an environment where it is OK to fail

Creating an environment where it is OK to fail takes time and effort to develop: it is in the language that we use with students; it is in the daily lesson after lesson interactions with students; and it is even down to the displays that we have in our classrooms. How do you talk to your students? Are the words you use and your tonality supportive or derogatory? Are students supported to thrive in your lesson though your interactions, or are they belittled and shamed?

The first step is to get students to recognise when they are displaying a fixed mindset. To help with this you need to educate them in the language. Do they know what fixed and growth mindsets are? Ask them and discuss with them the importance of having a growth mindset, sharing the idea that if they are struggling it's not because they can't do it – it's just that they can't do it yet! The language we use with students can be incredibly powerful, especially at times of vulnerability such as when they are answering questions in front of the class. Using 'yet' supports the students to know that it does not mean that they will never be able to get the answers right, or improve in geography, rather that they are only part way along their learning journey and it is not over . . . yet.

Use displays and refer to them often when you catch students using fixed mindset language. Having a display board specifically for growth mindset can be an additional resource to reinforce your message. For example, my display contains the information shown in Figure 5.1.

Having looked at what we can do to foster a growth mindset so that students feel more confident in engaging with questions, the next challenge is to establish how we, as teachers, develop the habits to engage as many students as possible, consistently lesson after lesson – and not just the high-attaining students, but all students.

1% better

There are 195 days in the average academic year.

If we can be 1% better every day we are at school, by the end of the year we can be 7% better than we are now!

What would that look like?

The power of yet

I can't do this … yet.

I don't know … yet.

This doesn't make sense … yet.

I haven't passed … yet.

I don't understand … yet.

The language of growth mindset

Instead of ...	Try thinking...
I'm no good at this.	What can I do to understand? What am I missing?
I can't do geography.	I'm not going to give up at this.
I give up.	I'll use strategies that I used in the past.
I'll never be as smart as her.	I'm going to figure out what she does and try it.
I can't make it any better.	If this was the best piece of work I'd ever done, what else would it include?
This is too hard.	But I know I can work it out if I take my time and think clearly.
I don't know what to put.	Let's make a start and I know other ideas will flow into my head.

Figure 5.1 Growth mindset display

'No passengers'

'No passengers' is an approach designed to make sure that you do not have a class of passive learners, all sitting waiting for the time to tick by. This means that all students participate and therefore it matters little whether or not students have their hands up. An important feature of outstanding questioning is making sure that all students are involved and that there are no passengers in your lesson. Thus all students have to concentrate and listen because they may have to answer a question. This technique aims to eliminate the attitude of 'well, he never asks me so I don't have to pay attention.' 'No passengers' requires that all students contribute a 'good' answer (i.e. an answer with which you are satisfied and not an 'I don't know' response). It is vital that you tackle the 'I don't know' response, and that students are not allowed to get away with this as a standard response to avoid contributing to the lesson, or because they are not confident in answering. We will look at ways to tackle this.

Here are six techniques to tackle students saying 'I don't know', and to ensure that all students participate in your questioning sessions:

1 **'Give it some thought. I'm coming back to you.'** This gives the student thinking time: it may be that time is all that is required for the student to process the question and then come back with a response, but this also

allows time for the student to look in their books, or for a friend to whisper the answer to them. In my opinion, as long as it is not a test, it is acceptable for them to do this. The required outcome is that the student gives a 'good' answer to the question and feels successful in that moment. Your praise will help to build confidence, which will in turn promote more engagement and greater willingness to contribute in other question and answer sessions. 'Give it some thought' instructs the student to consider his/her answers rather than shouting out the first idea which comes to mind; this should result in a more thoughtful and high-quality answer.

2   **'No rush, have a think.'** If nothing else, this statement reminds me, as the teacher, that students need time to process questions to be able to formulate an answer. There has been a wealth of research on 'wait time', and it is believed that, on average, teachers allow between 0.7 and 1.4 seconds response time before answering the question themselves or asking somebody else. A moment of silence is not to be feared but encouraged, as it gives the student the opportunity to formulate a logical response, helping to build the growth mindset mentioned previously. Students become more comfortable with the silence as they think of a coherent response. It also helps to reduce the amount of speculative responses given to questions. It reduces the incidence of students merely saying the first thing that enters their head, as they know you will quickly move on after the answer whether the answer be right or wrong.

3   **'I'm going to ask you . . . in a minute so get thinking.'** Giving extra thinking time and pre-warning the students that they are going to be asked a question allows them to rehearse the answer in their head, or to find the answer in their book if necessary. This is a good question stem for students with low confidence, or those who rarely contribute answers, giving them the necessary time to prepare themselves. If students are particularly low in confidence you may well have reassured them, prior to the question and answer session, that their work was to a good standard and that their answers were right. This reduces the fear of failure for the students, making them far more willing to contribute. Obviously this reassurance can be withdrawn as the students' confidence and resilience grows.

4   **'What did . . . say?'** This question is posed to a student who has stated that he/she does not know the answer. The student then has the opportunity to experience success, developing his/her listening skills and ultimately realising that he/she cannot opt out of giving an answer or contributing to the class discussion.

5 **'You've heard two answers, which one do you like the best?' 'Why?'** This again involves engaging with other students' responses. It requires students to use listening skills and a higher level of thinking to interpret and justify which answer they consider to be better, and the reasons why. Students may be encouraged to state which part of the answer was the best, for example: ideas were linked, key terms were used, the answer was backed up with evidence. You may wish to push further to ask 'Which ideas did they link?' 'Which key terms were used?' 'Can you define those key terms for us?'

6 **'Guess . . .'** Putting 'guess' at the beginning of a question makes students more comfortable in answering without worrying about making a mistake. The teacher's tonality is key to this. If you ask students to 'guess' in a light and airy fashion, as if you are not bothered whether they are right or wrong, the fear of failure dissolves and thus student participation increases. This is one technique which will often highlight the biggest misconceptions. If the teacher's tonality and expression/body language are all correct this can be the most comfortable setting for students to either ask follow-up questions or to feel most accepting of failure. It is at these times that misconceptions or gaps in knowledge and understanding can be most transparent.

These six techniques need to be practised and rehearsed so that they become habits. You will then not need to think consciously about which 'no passengers' technique you need to use; rather you will be unconsciously competent at it and thus be working at a level of automaticity. The whole point of 'no passengers' is to get all students willingly contributing to class discussions, and question and answer sessions, so that in time you will not need these techniques as much. For that to happen, students need to feel successful and for their fear of failure to reduce. This is all achieved through the chemical processes in our brains. If the questions are pitched at the right level they offer just the right level of challenge, and when students are successful at answering them they receive a release of dopamine. Dopamine is one of the 'happy' chemicals; it's the same chemical released when we achieve something or tick something off our 'to do' list. It creates a sense of achievement – so the more students are able to experience it, the more likely they are to want to replicate that feeling in our lessons, and thus answer more questions.

Purposes of questioning

The questions that you ask your students will be used for a variety of purposes, such as to measure what they already know or to engage and encourage students to develop their geographical literacy. Do you use them to assess the level of understanding and then to clarify this understanding? Do you use them to challenge? Questions should be aimed at developing the students, pushing them to their limits and beyond their comfort zone, stimulating their thinking so that they, in turn, come up with their own questions.

Measuring

Measuring or barometer questions are used to gauge the level of skills, knowledge and understanding your students may already have on a given topic. These will tend to be closed questions, asked at the start of the lesson, related to the lesson title or learning question. Common question stems may include:

- What do you know about . . . ?
- What is . . . ?
- When . . . ?
- How is . . . ?
- Do you know . . . ?
- When did . . . ?
- How does . . . happen?

These question stems often elicit one-word answers or limited-detail responses from the students. They require a limited amount of knowledge application or deep thinking. However, they give you a quick snapshot of the current level of understanding of a topic for selected students. They by no means tell you the level of understanding of all the students in your class. However, using closed questions does have several advantages: it is a quick process; it allows you to evaluate the level of knowledge of certain students; and it provides you with the flexibility to offer appropriate challenge to the students in the lesson. There is little point in delivering a lesson if even one child at the end states 'I knew all that before.' For example, if you are teaching the students to draw pie charts related to their fieldwork you may need to explain the whole process to them, going into detail about the 360° in a circle, and how to calculate percentages. However, with a few measuring questions you may realise that the students have a clear grasp of how to draw pie charts from the work in maths, and it may require you to simply recap on the main points or pair up 'experts' with some students who may struggle.

Challenge

Questions that challenge students will most often be open questions aimed at developing the students' understanding and requiring them to think more deeply in order to provide a logical answer. The challenge questions I use in lessons are a combination of exam command words and question stems from Bloom's Taxonomy. I am confident that you are familiar with Bloom's Taxonomy: it is a hierarchy of questions classified according to their level of cognitive demand, starting from low-level knowledge questions such as who, what, when, label, name, to high-level evaluation questions such as prioritise, argue, justify. There is an obvious overlap between examination command words and Bloom's Taxonomy, and it is important for students to recognise and understand these terms to help them to improve their performance in exams. Recognising the hierarchy of questions will allow you to differentiate your questions to the students. Whilst it is necessary to differentiate your questions, it is also important to offer appropriate challenge as well. Challenge questions should aim to do just that: challenge. They need to be pitched at a high enough level to stretch the students' comfort zone, making them think more deeply to find the answer; they should stimulate their thinking so that they may even look at previously unconsidered possibilities. Table 5.1 contains a range of command words and Bloom's Taxonomy questions that I use regularly in my lessons. This is just a sample; a full list of Bloom's question stems can be found on the Internet. The command words for GCSE exams are shown in bold.

In addition to challenging the students' knowledge and understanding of a concept or a topic, it is important to develop their examination skills. This involves reflection on answers given in the lesson. If I tell a student that he/she

Table 5.1 Question stems

Low level	Mid level	High level (deep thinking)
Describe . . .	Explain . . .	Argue . . .
Label . . .	Outline . . .	Assess . . .
Name . . .	Compare . . .	Contrast . . .
Define . . .	How would . . .	Justify . . .
List . . .	Annotate . . .	Suggest . . .
How is . . .	Account for . . .	Prioritise . . .
Who, what, when, where	Comment . . .	How would you solve/improve . . .
Choose . . .	Give reasons . . .	Evaluate . . .
Pick out . . .	Can you link . . .	Recommend . . .

has given a good answer, I want the students to know why it was a good answer, and to dissect the elements of the answer so that they all recognise good practice. Following is a selection of questions I use to develop students' thinking around responses:

- 'Good answer, can you tell me why that was a good answer?'
- 'How could we improve that answer?'
- 'If that was an exam question and answer, how many marks would you award it? Why?'
- 'Can you link that idea to another?'
- 'Can you link that idea to another part of the course?'
- 'What would a model answer include?'

Assessing

Verbal questioning to assess the students' knowledge and understanding involves thoughtful question selection and also carefully listening to the students' responses. It necessitates holding out until you are fully happy with the answer given by the student or students. The purpose is to clarify the students' understanding and – as all the students are listening – they all get to put their ideas together to model an excellent answer. I will often then ask students to write a response to my question, having heard from the class. You can support low-attaining students by putting a selection of key terms on the board to support them. Following are two examples of my questioning technique before and after developing my questioning skills around assessing students' understanding.

A typical dialogue before developing my questioning habit

'What are the problems of favelas?'

'Bad water'

'Yes, that's right, contaminated water which leads to diseases. What is another problem?'

A typical dialogue after developing my questioning habit

'Susan, in a minute I'm going to ask you to prioritise the problems of living in a favela; do you understand what I mean by prioritise?'

'What I think is the worst thing first?'

'Correct.'

'So Susan, what do you consider the worst problem is of living in a favela?'

'Bad water.'

'Susan, can you give me that answer in a sentence?'

'The worst problem of living in a favela is bad water.'

'OK Michael, can you give me a better word for *bad* water?'

'Contaminated.'

'Superb.'

'So Susan, can you have another go?'

'The worst problem of living in a favela is the contaminated water.'

'Jane, can you add to the answer, link ideas together?'

'The worst problem of living in a favela is the contaminated water, as it can lead to diseases.'

'Such as . . . ?'

'Cholera.'

'Fantastic. Stephen, what was good about the answer we've just heard?'

'She linked the ideas together and used examples of a disease.'

'Fab. Ryan, you're going to hear another answer now and I want you to evaluate and decide which answer you think is best and why. Kate, what would you say is the worst problem of living in a favela and why?'

This style of questioning has a powerful effect on the students' knowledge and understanding of the content of the lesson. The benefits are:

- They learn how to structure a good oral answer that they can then translate onto paper.
- They learn to include key terminology and how to extend their vocabulary.
- They learn from each other what makes a good answer and what a good answer includes.
- They acquire new knowledge from each other.
- They share ideas and knowledge.
- There is opportunity to question each other or for the teacher to clarify their understanding.

Assessing learning: hinge questions

Another approach to assessing students' knowledge is the use of hinge questions. Hinge questions assess the students' understanding at a 'hinge point' in the lesson (i.e. a point at which it is necessary for the students to know a particular concept or idea before they are able to move on). The key idea of hinge questions is that they allow you to gather information from the whole class, so that you can address any misconceptions or remedy gaps in their knowledge or understanding before progressing with the lesson or topic. This is achieved by using (in most cases) multiple-choice questions for the students to answer.

Creating effective hinge questions

1   The hinge question should directly relate to the lesson's learning question or at least support the learning question. This ensures that the hinge question is essential for further progression, rather than an 'add on' or subsidiary idea.

2   The hinge question should be a quick-response question (no more than 2 minutes) so that the teacher can swiftly assess student responses, thus ascertaining the level of understanding before moving on.

3   The responses given will allow the teacher to modify his/her teaching. Do the students need to clarify or can they proceed with the lesson?

Hinge questions can be a very useful diagnostic tool to establish the level of student understanding. The trick to making good hinge questions is to create multiple-choice questions that have a number of plausible answers. Hinge questions do not have to be used in large numbers; in fact, one question may suffice for students to demonstrate the key concept you are trying to embed before you move on.

The logistics of hinge questions can require some thought. How will you get all your students to answer the question? You could use the back of the students' exercise books and they could hold up their answer, you could use whiteboards, coloured cards or electronic tablets. There are also apps that can be downloaded that allow your students to 'vote' for answers.

Questioning to improve geographical literacy

As discussed in Chapter 8, literacy in geography is vital if students are to be successful, and literacy standards can be improved through questioning.

This improvement can be achieved by students improving their oracy, which in turn should translate into improvements in their written work. The idea being, 'If they can speak it, then they can write it.' With that in mind, if we demand a high standard of oracy then we should expect to see these high standards convert into their written work. This can be achieved by making the three following statements a habit when questioning students:

1   'Give me that answer in a sentence.' This develops the student's ability to write in full sentences.

2   'Can you give me a better word or another word for . . .' This extends and builds the student's vocabulary.

3   'Use the proper standard English thank you.' This ensures that the students are reminded to always use the correct standard English in lessons and within their written work.

These three statements can help your students to refine their answers, and require them to think more deeply than when they simply give one-word answers. If you can make using these statements a habit, so too will the students develop their own habits of answering in full standard English sentences, with an array of key terms and impressive vocabulary.

Questioning strategies to improve student oracy

Think pair share

This strategy involves asking the class a question and then allowing students to discuss the answer in pairs. They may consult their books or resources and then orally rehearse what they are going to say. After a specified time, you ask one of the pairs to respond to the question.

Pose pause pounce bounce

This technique is attributed to Ross McGill and it works in the following way:

1   Pose: pose a question to the class that requires some thought rather than a low-level closed question.

2   Pause: pause to give the class thinking time or to discuss their response in pairs.

3   Pounce: pounce on a student to give an answer.

4 Bounce: bounce the response to another student in the class and ask him/her to reflect on the original answer given. Was it correct? Could anything be added to it?

Student questions

If we are doing our job well and we are engaging and enthusing our students within an environment where it is OK to make mistakes, then one would hope that the students themselves would be willing to ask questions. This can be achieved in a number of ways.

Questioning culture

First, I would expect students to ask any questions they have regarding anything I have been teaching, whether in the lesson at the time or from previous lessons. I would expect this because I have worked hard to create a culture of questioning, for the students to know that there are no silly questions that cannot be asked if they are to clear up misconceptions or to clarify their understanding. If you have created an environment where students feel safe to ask questions, without fear or the threat of ridicule, then students will be far more willing to ask.

Pre-topic questions

When you start a new topic, give a short explanation of what you will be studying or show a short introductory clip of the topic. Then ask the students to write down questions on sticky notes that they would like to be answered by the end of the topic. Once all the students have written down their questions (I normally insist that each student must come up with at least three questions), then these questions can be stuck on a board or area of the classroom. When I get the opportunity I then look through the questions and find out what the students want to know. In most cases their questions will match the scheme of work I will be teaching, but sometimes there will be a question on an aspect of the topic I had not considered. This gives you the chance to engage with these questions, and you and the class can discover the answers together. As I move through the lessons I will refer to the questions and take them off the board as they are addressed. I may well do this at the start of the lesson, announcing that today we will be answering Ryan's question, or at the end of a lesson I may refer to the board and state that today we have answered Martyn's and Laura's questions.

Question formulation

This activity can be a group, pair or individual challenge. I find it works best with groups of three, so all members of the group are involved, and I use this technique with students from Year 7 up to Year 13.

1   Decide on a focus area. This could be as wide as a topic area, for example 'Urbanisation', or a narrower focus, for example 'The problems of megacities in Low Income Countries'.

2   The students then write down as many questions as they can think of in a minute. Introduce this as a competition; the point is for them to create questions rather to stop and think of the merits of each individual question. At this stage it is all about volume. You can get the whole class to stand up and then sit down as you go through the number of questions. 'Sit down all of you who got ten questions, eleven, twelve.' Then give the students one further minute to repeat the exercise and again find out which the winning group was in the second round.

3   Once the groups have a long list of questions then they need to sort their questions into categories. These could be open or closed questions, silly and sensible, questions worth six or less marks and questions worth six or more marks.

4   Students select their best three questions.

You may wish to provide the groups with question stems and command words, depending upon the setting. I would expect my GCSE and A Level students to be using the appropriate command words to help them formulate their questions. At Key Stage 3 you may expect to see more low-level closed questions. However there is nothing stopping you from giving the question stems to lower years to see what they can come up with. The questions that the students have produced can be used in the lesson, or you may even want to use their questions in an assessment or in a mock exam paper.

As discussed earlier, questioning is a cornerstone of outstanding teaching and it is a skill that many teachers feel they do very well. Yet questioning is an art that gets better with refined practice. The lesson plan template in Figure 3.1 includes a box showing questioning stems that I had stuck to my desk for several years, and to which I would refer throughout my lessons. It acted as a cue to remind me what I need to say at specific points during questioning sessions. I looked at it during lessons five times a day for months. It was that constant practice that helped to develop my techniques into a deeply ingrained habit, and these I now use with total automaticity. This does not mean that I stop trying to get better; I have refined and improved my template to remind me to refer to command words more in my teaching, and I will continue to refer to this template until that also has become a habit. Figure 5.2 refers to the key points to improve your questioning technique. Differentiation for all

Questioning in a nutshell

- Get ALL students involved in the questioning process. If they don't know the answer get them to comment on the answers they have heard or to repeat back the correct answer.
- Develop growth mindset through questioning.
- Use command words when questioning.
- Differentiate your questions by using Bloom's Taxonomy.
- Develop oracy through questioning: have high expectations and insist that standards are followed.
- Get students to ask more questions. Reinforce this by saying 'You asked great questions today' rather than 'Good work.'

Figure 5.2 Questioning in a nutshell

CHAPTER 6

Differentiation
How to offer appropriate challenge for all

Differentiation is the way in which teachers respond to the variety of students' needs in their class, how they accommodate those needs so that all students are appropriately challenged and thus have the best possible chance to learn. The challenge for us as teachers is to consider how we accommodate all those different students, each with his/her own set of unique needs.

Each student has his/her own story to tell, with unique life experiences, level of self-esteem and confidence, skill set and motivations. It is this complex scenario of thirty different minds (approximately) that can make differentiation so difficult to administer. Yet it needn't be. Differentiation doesn't mean thirty different worksheets or continuous rejigging of ability groups. Put simply, differentiation comes down to three main strands: modify the content (what's being taught), the process (how it's taught) and the product (how students demonstrate what they have learnt). What is paramount when considering differentiation is to ensure that all students are adequately supported and appropriately challenged, regardless of prior attainment. If we are able to achieve this, then the classroom will be enhanced with improvements in participation, motivation, behaviour and progress.

Challenge choice

This technique is dependent upon the content you have taught the students previously. A basic structure may be that, having delivered some topic content, you then ask the students to select a question or questions from the differentiated challenge grid, an example of which is shown in Table 6.1. In this scenario, students have been learning about Brazilian favelas. They then have the opportunity to select two questions from the challenge grid to answer. This freedom of choice increases engagement and motivation for the activity from the students. At this point I would remind the class that they should be

Table 6.1 Challenge choice

Describe the features of a favela.	Prioritise the problems of the favelas.	What do you think the favelas will be like in ten years' time? Why?
Explain the problems of life in a favela.	Explain how life in the favelas can be improved.	Link ideas together to explain what would happen if the government decided to bulldoze all the favelas down.

challenging themselves and not selecting the questions that they find the easiest. In my experience, having given that instruction students rarely choose the 'easy' question. Having selected their questions the students can get on with the process of answering them to the best of their ability. Once the students have had an appropriate amount of time you could bring the class back by saying, 'OK, let's hear your answers to this question. Who answered this one?' Then all students have the opportunity to contribute to the discussion whether they answered that specific question or not.

The advantage of this technique is that it offers a range of challenge for all students. Lower-attaining students can access the questions with stems such as 'describe' and 'explain', having previously learnt about favelas. High-attaining students have the opportunity to consider the social, economic, political and environmental costs of the government bulldozing the favelas, a truly high-end challenge. As a teacher the question grid gives you a range of options. You could direct students to answer certain questions: for example, students who are working at a developing level can answer the questions in the first column whilst you may instruct higher-attaining students to answer the questions in the third column. You may ask the students to answer one question from each column and add more questions to the grid, thus offering progression through the lesson. I often mix the questions up and present them all in the same colour, and ask students to differentiate the questions themselves, giving them the ownership to answer whichever questions they want, challenging themselves to achieve and succeed.

This technique offers a wealth of possibilities: for example, you could offer just three questions or nine, and they could be exam questions or questions that the students generate themselves. You can tell the students which are the harder questions or you could ask them to work it out for themselves.

The question/verb stems are derived from Bloom's Taxonomy; they offer increasing levels of challenge to develop students' thinking and their understanding of a topic. Table 6.2 presents a sample of question/verb stems that could be used, crudely put into three columns of challenge.

Table 6.2 Bloom's Taxonomy question stems

Low challenge	Medium challenge	High challenge
Describe . . .	Explain . . .	Prioritise . . .
Label . . .	Outline . . .	How would you solve/improve . . . ?
Measure . . .	Discuss . . .	
Select . . .	Compare . . .	Can you predict . . . ?
Sketch . . .	Classify . . .	Justify . . .
Name . . .	Summarise . . .	What would happen if . . . ?
Pick out . . .	What is the main idea about . . . ?	How could you test . . . ?
Who, what, when, where, why?		Can you offer an alternative . . . ?
Define . . .	What is the pattern of . . . ?	How would you measure/rate . . . ?
List . . .	Connect . . .	Why do you think . . . is not/is important?
Highlight . . .	Translate . . .	
	Can you link . . . ?	

Photo challenge questions

Photographic stimuli are commonly used in geography examinations, both at GCSE and A Level. This technique aims to develop students' ability to respond to exam-style questions, whilst also improving their skills of photograph interpretation. As shown in Figure 6.1 a photograph or picture is placed in the middle of the question sheet and then four questions are arranged around the photo at different levels of challenge. The students can be either directed to answer specific questions, or they themselves can choose which question or questions to answer. As previously mentioned, I ask the students to challenge themselves to the best of their ability. The remaining questions can be answered in the following ways:

- Ask the students to find and teach each other the answers to the questions.
- Students can use their books or textbooks to find the answers to the remaining questions.
- Students are given the questions as a homework activity.
- Ask the students to find the answers using their laptop, tablet or mobile phone.

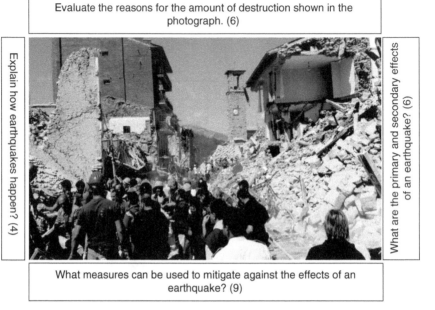

Evaluate the reasons for the amount of destruction shown in the photograph. (6)

Explain how earthquakes happen? (4)

What are the primary and secondary effects of an earthquake? (6)

What measures can be used to mitigate against the effects of an earthquake? (9)

Figure 6.1 Photo challenge questions

Challenge corner

This is a dedicated corner of the classroom where students can go to access a range of resources, aimed to challenge the students further or provide resources to support their learning. This area caters to those students who have finished their work and require an extra challenge or extension activity, as well as provides support for low-attaining students who may need that additional assistance to complete their challenge. My challenge corner has the following resources.

- Twitter templates: students who have completed their work can write a tweet to explain what they have learnt during the lesson or how they have made progress with their work.

- Storyboard: students can complete a six-frame storyboard to describe and explain what they have learnt during the lesson.

- Diamond rank: students diamond-rank the key content they have learnt, prioritising their knowledge by putting their most important piece of knowledge at the top of the diamond and the least important at the bottom.

- Mobile phone template: this is easily one of the favourites with the students. They write a text message to a friend in text language about what they have learnt during the lesson.

- Self-assessment sheets: these may be generic or specific to a particular topic or year group. Essentially they could be success criteria against which the students can assess themselves. The students have the opportunity to comment on what they have learnt and on what has gone well, and to reflect on what they need to do to improve their performance.

- Literacy mats: these mats help students with their extended writing. They provide students with lists of key connectives and also spellings of geographical terminology.

- Generic writing frames: these provide guidance for students on how to complete extended writing challenges, breaking down the piece of writing into what to include in each paragraph.

- Textbooks: I offer a range of textbooks from Key Stage 3 to 5. Therefore students can refer to the textbook that we have been currently using in connection with the topic, but they can also look at the textbook from another key stage to challenge themselves to learn more about the same topic.

- Challenge questions: these are generic questions or challenges that the students can select and complete. They simply pick a card from the envelope and attempt to answer the question or complete the challenge. Following are examples from twenty generic challenges that I use.

  ○ Write down six things you have learnt today; then put them in order of importance.

  ○ Write four multiple choice questions to test your friend's knowledge of the lesson.

  ○ How could you improve your performance next lesson?

  ○ What do you know now that you did not know at the start of the lesson?

  ○ Swap your exercise book with someone else who has finished and assess it. What have they done well? What could they do to improve their work?

  ○ Design a set of symbols to represent what you have learnt in today's lesson.

  ○ Make your own poster of the key things you have learnt so far during this topic.

  ○ Choose five keywords we have used so far during this topic and write down their definitions.

Progress tracker

This activity is hugely engaging and gives both the students and you the teacher a clear indication of progress within your lesson. Create a display in your room that can show three distinct levels. These levels could be developing (lower stage), consolidating (middle stage) and extending (higher stage). I use a picture of a mountain side, with the bottom section representing base camp or *developing* and the top representing the peak or *extending*. Students then either write their name on a sticky note or you may ask them to draw a small picture of themselves. This activity then involves students moving their name or picture on the display as they progress.

This challenge involves students working with resources and questions pitched at different levels. All students can begin with the developing questions: these are aimed at consolidating the students' skills and knowledge, and ensuring they have mastered the skill or content before moving on to the secure questions, and then finally the extending questions. The consolidating questions offer increased rigour and challenge, aimed at getting the students to link ideas and apply what they have learnt. The extending questions are the higher level questions aimed at stretching the students to think more deeply about the topic, before applying their knowledge and understanding to the question.

Some students may feel confident that they can answer the 'developing questions' and therefore select a higher level question. In essence the students are deciding the level they wish to work at. This obviously comes with a caveat that you may need to direct students to a particular set of questions. This activity gives both you and the students a range of opportunities. The activity can be used in any of the following ways:

- All students must answer at least one question from each of the three categories.
- Students select which questions they choose to answer.
- The teacher directs students to particular questions.
- The questions are linked to a prior assessment and thus students must answer those questions they have gotten wrong from a previous test.
- The students must reach a certain tally of marks before moving on to the next level. This may be peer, self or teacher marked. For example: 'You need to score 10 on the developing questions before you can move on to the consolidating questions.'

Once the students have completed the question, they can move their name or picture of themselves on the display. This shows both you and the students how they are progressing in the lesson. It is a clear visual representation of who is where in relation to progress, which allows you to swiftly intervene and support those students in need, allowing the rest of the class to progress with their own learning.

The example worksheets shown in Figures 6.2–6.5 are based on river landscapes. You may want to use this strategy as a revision tool, yet it can be used when the students are part way through the topic. The high-level questions in Figure 6.5 may represent independent learning, where you require the students to research and find the answers for themselves prior to you having taught it. Students are given the relevant worksheet and then they work on the questions you wish them to answer. Once completed, depending upon your instruction they can check their answers from the textbook or other resources you may use. They could use a prepared mark scheme or they may mark each other's work. Alternatively they could ask you, allowing you to see their work and check that it is correct before letting the students move on to the next challenge or sheet.

Differentiation through questioning

Although questioning is discussed in Chapter 5, it is worth repeating that rigorous and challenging questions are vital to differentiation in the classroom. Differentiated questioning allows low-attaining students to access the lesson, gain success and challenge their thinking, while high-attaining students can be stretched with high order analytical reasoning. When considering the level of questioning to use, there is little better reference available than Bloom's Taxonomy which provides the foundation for much of the questioning that takes place in classrooms up and down the country. It works as a hierarchy of challenge, beginning with low-order questions such as what and how, and moving to high-order thinking such as justify and evaluate.

Lead learners

Selecting students to be 'lead learners' has a number of benefits. The remaining students in the class have somebody to refer to if they wish to ask questions, or if they need clarity on what they are supposed to be doing. They can ask the lead learners if their work is correct or what they need to add to improve their

Developing

Success Criteria

1. I can define the processes of erosion and transportation.
2. I can label the features of the upper course.
3. I can catagorise the feature of the river course.

Challenge 1

Define the following terms:

- Hydraulic action
- Abrasion
- Attrition
- Solution

Challenge 2

What are the four processes of transportation? Write them down with their definition.

Challenge 3: List all the features and processes found in the three parts of the river course.

Upper course	Middle course	Lower course

Challenge 4: Sketch the photograph above and label the river's features you can see.

Challenge 5: Sketch the cross profile of a river channel and describe the processes at work (erosion, transportation, deposition).

Progress: Before moving on, check your answers.

Read it: check your answers in the text book.

Mark it: mark your work with the mark scheme.

Peer it: get a partner to check and mark your work.

Teach it: get your teacher to check your work.

Teach what you have learnt to your partner.

Figure 6.2 Differentiation sheet (developing)

Consolidating

Success Criteria

- I know how the river changes downstream.
- I can label and interpret storm hydrographs.
- I know how river features are formed.

Prior knowledge

You know:

- Processes of erosion
- Processes of transportation
- Features of a river valley

Challenge 1:

Account for the changes that occur to the river's cross and long profile as you move downstream.

Challenge 2:

With the aid of a diagram explain the formation of a waterfall. Use a case study to support your answer.

Challenge 3:

Sketch the diagrams below and add annotations to explain the formation of ox bow lakes.

Progress: Before moving on check your answers.

Read it: check your answers in the text book.

Mark it: mark your work with the mark scheme.

Peer it: get a partner to check and mark your work.

Teach it: get your teacher to check your work.

Challenge 4: Give reasons for the shape of the two hydrographs.

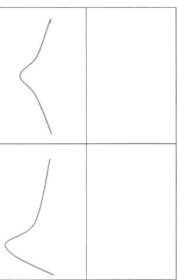

Figure 6.3 Differentiation sheet (consolidating)

Extending

Success Criteria:

- I know the physical and human causes of floods.
- I know and understand the causes, effects and management strategies of flooding.
- I can recognise river features from ordnance survey maps.

Prior Knowledge: You know:

- Processes of erosion and transportation.
- River features and how they are formed.
- The reasons for and features of storms.

Challenge 1: What are the physical and human causes of floods? Complete the table below.

Physical	Human

Challenge 2: compare different flood management strategies by completing the table below.

Strategy	Benefit	Cost
Hard engineering: dams and reservoirs		
Channel straightening		
Embankments		
Flood relief channels		
Soft engineering: flood warnings		
Flood plain zoning		
Planting trees and restoration		

Progress: Before moving on check your answers.

Read it: check your answers in the text book.

Mark it: mark your work with the mark scheme.

Peer it: get a partner to check and mark your work.

Teach it: get your teacher to check your work.

Teach what you have learnt to your partner

Figure 6.4 Differentiation sheet (extending)

Extending 2

Challenge 4: Using the word cloud below create your own GCSE style questions. You can add words to help you make your questions. Then answer them!

Success Criteria:

- I can describe and explain river features created by both erosion and deposition.
- I can identify landforms and explain processes that occur along a river's long profile.
- I can evaluate both hard and soft engineering flood protection methods and relate these to a case study example.
- I recognise GCSE command words and I understand how they are used to assess my knowledge of the topic.

Challenge 1: Describe and explain the formation of interlocking spurs and gorges.

Challenge 2: Using an example of a river valley, identify its major landforms created by erosion and deposition.

Challenge 3: With reference to an example, explain and justify the flood protection methods employed to control flooding in that area.

Progress: Before moving on check your answers.

Read it: check your answers in the text book.

Mark it: mark your work with the mark scheme.

Peer it: get a partner to check and mark your work.

Teach it: get your teacher to check your work.

> Teach what you have learnt to your partner.

Figure 6.5 Differentiation sheet (extending 2)

work. Peer assistance is often more welcome than that gained from the teacher. This may be because their fellow classmates are friends who can support them, or it may be because they see the lead learners as non-judgemental. The lead learners benefit as they need to have properly mastered the topic or content being taught to then be able to support and teach their classmates. Teaching their classmates requires a depth of understanding: they not only have to understand the content thoroughly but they must also be able to convey that knowledge to others. It is vital that your lead learners have fully mastered the skill or content you are asking them to deliver; if they have not, this can lead to misconceptions, confusion and a delay in progress. It is therefore important that you are confident with the lead learners' knowledge and understanding first. For the teacher it is a benefit to have students who the others can ask and refer to, thus freeing you up so that you can work with those students who may be struggling with a particular challenge.

How it can work in practice

If we use the example of any end-of-topic test, having completed the assessment the students receive their papers for feedback. As the teacher I then go through the answers, asking students to contribute to the class discussion as we discover the correct answers and they annotate their papers with the feedback I am giving. Having completed my initial feedback I can now use the lead learners. Since I have marked their test papers, I am fully aware of who has mastered the topic or at least key parts of the topic; I then send the lead learners to one of several desks or work stations. The remaining students are then sent to work with the lead learners to improve aspects of their assessment. This gives them the opportunity to have another attempt at certain questions, knowing that they can ask their lead learner what they need to include to improve their work, or they can ask any questions they wish to clear up any misconceptions. The lead learners are tasked with teaching their particular group part of the assessment again. The lead learners' particular strength will be matched with the weaknesses of the group they have been tasked to teach. For example, after students complete an assessment on rivers I may set up the following work stations:

- Map skills: lead learner 1 with students A, B, C, D and E
- Formation of waterfalls: lead learner 2 with students F, G, H, I and J
- Interpretation of hydrographs: lead learner 3 with students K, L, M, N and O
- Flood management: lead learner 4 with students P, Q, R, S and T

I am then free to work with another group which may have different needs. This may be an underachieving group or a high attaining group which requires additional stretch and challenge.

The possibilities are endless, as are the combinations of how to organise this in your class. You may want to split the class into groups before you give your whole class feedback, to see what the students have learnt whilst at their work stations. This new knowledge can then be shared during the feedback session.

Other approaches using lead learners

- Lead learners may support other students once they have completed their challenge.
- Lead learners may produce their own teaching material and resources to support others.
- Lead learners may organise students when working in groups.
- Lead learners may act as partners for weaker students, being their first port of call; the lead learners have the responsibility of making sure that their partner completes the work to a good standard.

I would not envisage using lead learners in every lesson. As the teacher I will often prefer to be the first reference point for students so that I can judge misconceptions within the class, and thus remedy any issues or problems arising. Also, I would not always have the same students as leads; there is an obvious tendency for your lead learners to be your most able students. However, students have different skills in different areas, and thus I would aim to make all students lead learners at some point. In fact it can be beneficial to have those students who have struggled most to be lead learners, as they have had to tackle the problems of understanding the skills or content themselves, and therefore they can pass on this wisdom. More able students sometimes struggle to comprehend why other students 'just don't get it'.

As you would expect, the title of lead learner comes with a degree of prestige; whether the students like to admit to it or not, they always enjoy the role. It gives a boost to their self-esteem, releases serotonin and makes them feel better about themselves. To aid this I give my students a lanyard with a badge saying 'lead learner'; this again reinforces their role and adds to its significance within the classroom.

Pre-topic test

An important aspect of differentiation is to know the students' starting points. From this you will be able to plan effectively to meet the range of needs you may have in your class. Rather than guessing or assuming what the students know, begin each topic with a pre-test. Table 6.3 is an example of a pre-test created on tropical rainforests. This does not have to involve reams of exam papers and marking but could simply be ten questions based on the key aspects of the course. The depth, length and nature of the test will depend upon the key stage and also what you want to discover about the students' knowledge. This simple device can save a lot of time and planning. For example, what is the point of teaching the water cycle to students if they already all know it? That time can be better spent learning something new or developing their knowledge, rather than going over pre-learned work.

Table 6.3 Example of a pre-test on the tropical rainforest

Tropical Rainforests Pre-test		
What do you already know about the tropical rainforests?		
Give your First Attempt In Learning in the F.A.I.L box. Don't worry if you don't know that answer at this point, it's all about having a go. Complete the Second Attempt In Learning box once your teacher has given feedback to you.		
Question	**F.A.I.L. Answer**	**S.A.I.L. Answer**
Where are the tropical rainforests located?		
Give the names of as many tropical rainforests as you can.		
What is the climate of the tropical rainforests?		
How have the plants adapted to the climate?		
What is deforestation?		
What are the causes of deforestation?		
What are the local impacts of deforestation?		
What are the global impacts of deforestation?		
What can be done to save the rainforests?		
What would you like to learn about during this topic?		

Sequencing mats

Sequencing mats can be very helpful for some low-attaining students who struggle to grasp key concepts or to link ideas together. The principle is that students have to sequence a number of pictures or cards into the correct order so that a process can be explained. You may wish to combine pictures and text to help the students access the task more easily. Do not feel that this requires you to laminate and cut out a whole host of different cards. The same outcome can be produced by asking the students themselves to collect or draw pictures or to write their own text boxes to be used in the activity. In fact I often ask the students to write on the desk using board pens that can be wiped off afterwards. This encourages them to be involved even more as in my experience the students always enjoy writing on the desks. They then construct a sequence of events or processes that create the final outcome you are challenging them to explain. Examples of when this can be used include:

- The formation of a waterfall
- The formation of sea stacks
- The events leading up to a tropical storm disaster
- The responses to an earthquake, volcano or flooding event
- The events leading up to a flood event
- The growth of tourism in a location related to the Butlers Model
- How a megacity has grown

There is such scope for this activity, and the visual and kinaesthetic nature of the activity makes it accessible and enjoyable for all. Students have to decide the order and sequence, and the decision making process often creates high-level thinking opportunities, with students debating exactly where pictures or text should go.

Quick ideas for 'outstanding' differentiation

Hopefully the range of strategies outlined in this chapter has increased your confidence when considering differentiation. As mentioned at the start of this chapter, differentiation is not about creating thirty different worksheets, but it is about knowing your students, knowing their needs and putting into place activities that challenge all your students. Following is a list of other strategies that can be used to aid differentiation in your classroom.

- When giving instructions ask your low-attaining students to repeat back their understanding of the challenge. This will check their understanding and ensure they are not off task once they start because they don't know what they are supposed to be doing.

- Use your seating plan to your advantage. Consider having low-attaining students next to middle-attaining students so that the low attainer can learn from a middle attainer who has to work hard to achieve. This also helps students to develop a positive work ethic.

- Have keywords displayed at the front of the classroom so the students can see them all the time.

- Have an open-ended task every lesson to stretch your most able students.

- Create different starting points for your students.

- Have specific questions you will ask specific students.

- Have an open door 'geography clinic' so students can drop in if they are stuck with a particular aspect of the course.

- Set individual targets when providing feedback.

- Give out different resources to support and challenge different students or groups of students: for example, give A Level textbooks to your high attainers to work from whilst you support the low attainers with Key Stage 3 and 4 textbooks.

- Have a range of support materials for students: writing frames, connective mats, keywords and definitions. Figure 6.6 highlights the key points of the chapter.

Differentiation in a nutshell

- It's all about appropriate challenge, so that **all** students can participate and progress
- Consider students having different starting points rather than them all doing the same
- Set up a 'challenge corner' to stretch your high attaining students and support you lower attaining students
- Use prior assessment to match challenges to student's needs
- Use lead learners to support their peers

Figure 6.6 Differentiation in a nutshell

CHAPTER 7

How to create curiosity and teach geography through enquiry

Curiosity in our students is the engine that drives deeper learning. It is the emotion that leads to exploratory behaviour and the desire to know more. In fact curiosity has been described as 'A powerful feeling that impels us forward until we find the information that will fill the gap in our knowledge' (Paul, 2013). Curiosity is linked to learning in two distinct ways. First, it is a key source of motivation – the curious student is motivated to fill the gap in his/her knowledge, striving to gain the information that will reduce the feeling of knowledge deprivation. Second, curiosity is powered by questions – and asking questions is essential to the development of knowledge and understanding.

Questions are the fundamental essence of curiosity and enquiry learning. Question generation is a skill; it is not the case that you merely ask students what they would like to know at the start of the topic, neither is it the case that you, as the teacher, should be putting questions into the students' mouths, as it were. However it is important to note that little can be gained by asking students to come up with questions that they can already answer; nor is it advisable to ask students to come up with questions when they have absolutely no knowledge of the topic in the first instance.

Curiosity requires some initial knowledge. Students cannot be curious about something of which they know nothing. Relatively minor input from the teacher can spark curiosity if students are provided with the opportunity to develop their own thinking, and thus their own questions. Far too often we are in such a hurry to impart our knowledge that we overlook the opportunities to allow students to question and think for themselves. In fact, if we slow down our delivery of the course content we can create the right conditions for curiosity to bloom. Research shows that curiosity increases with knowledge, so the more we know the more we want to know. Thus slowing down our pace may just provide the stimulus for the students to think for themselves on deeper and more complex issues or concepts.

Unfortunately, at times it may appear that the conditions in the classroom are not conducive to allow curiosity to flourish. With the demands to complete course content and the drive to improve standards, the opportunities for students to stop and think a while can be rare. Add to that the 'Google' generation where, with a few clicks, it appears that you can have any answer you want. All this has stifled that desire of students to discover information themselves. In fact, it is recognised that curiosity is a paradox in that once we have satisfied our curiosity about something we can feel a bit disappointed. It is the search that is the fun part, and the result is therefore a bit of an anticlimax. It is easy to find an answer by 'Googling it' but that doesn't give the rush of dopamine derived from the satisfaction of knowing we worked it out for ourselves.

How can we create curiosity and Enquiry Based Learning?

It will first be useful to define what I mean by Enquiry Based Learning. As with many teaching terms, 'enquiry' has become a hyperbole, the true meaning being lost in the myriad of discussions around its use in teaching. I believe the best definition is taken from Margret Roberts, an advocate of its use with geography and someone who has written widely about Enquiry Based Learning.

> *Enquiry Based Learning is a term used to cover a range of approaches in which students are actively engaged investigating questions and issues. Enquiry Based Learning has four essential characteristics:*
>
> 1 *It is question driven and encourages a questioning attitude towards knowledge.*
>
> 2 *Students study geographical data and sources of information as evidence.*
>
> 3 *Students make sense of information for themselves in order to develop understanding.*
>
> 4 *Students reflect on their learning.*
>
> (Roberts, 2013a: 50)

If we are to invest time into developing students' curiosity and pursuing answers through Enquiry Based Learning, then it is worth considering the planning necessary for it to be successful. The worst outcome would be for students to be given a free rein to discover answers to their questions, only to then come back after several lessons with a small mountain of papers, all copied and pasted from the Internet, with little or no knowledge gained. With considered planning and forethought it is possible to guide and support students, so that they can not only discover answers they wish to know, but they can also cultivate an appetite of curiosity and a desire to learn more. Figure 7.3 presents the enquiry process that can be useful for both students and teachers.

Stage 1: creating curiosity, the 'need to know'

If you want students to ask questions, first you must provide some sort of stimulus. What will you do to 'hook' the students into wanting to discover more? Following are a number of strategies that can be employed to stimulate questions from students.

Fake text messages: There are a number of websites that can be used to create fake messages (see Figure 7.1 for an example). You can then write a conversation that may be taking place in any geographical situation anywhere in the world. For example:

- Two residents of Pompeii as Vesuvius erupted
- Builders working on HS2
- Town planners in the Brazilian favelas
- Doctors treating malaria patients
- Flood victims
- Water droplets in the hydrological cycle

The possibilities are endless.

What's in the box? I have a box that I use to generate conversation, intrigue and curiosity. It is a black box, with a hole at one end, into which students can put their hands. Inside will be one or a number of objects related to the topic we are studying. The intention is that it creates questions as students try to identify the object. Once the object is revealed, it can then be used to create a second tranche of questions. For example, I recently used a few pieces of pumice stone that I had collected from a volcano. Students were inquisitive as to why the rocks were different colours, why the holes were different sizes, why the samples were different shapes and how the rocks were formed. In fact the questions seemed endless, and curiosity was certainly created. These questions can then form part of the enquiry that the students may wish to pursue.

Fill in the gaps: For this challenge pairs or small groups of students are given two pictures (one picture from the start of the story, scenario or setting, and one picture from the end). The challenge for the students is to 'fill

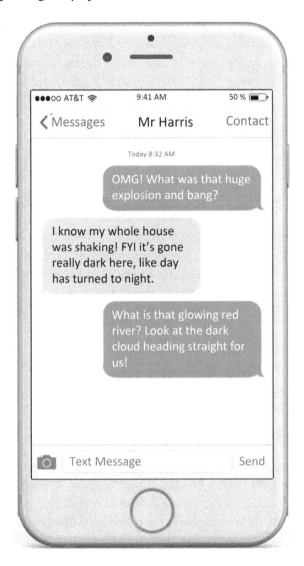

Figure 7.1 Fake text message generated with iOS7Text.com

the gap' and work out all the missing information that links the two pictures together. They may create a list of questions that they would like to answer, and then the students are given the opportunity to research and discover the answers.

Photographs: Just as pictures paint a thousand words, so too can they generate an abundance of questions. Whether the picture is a close-up of a geographical feature or a satellite image from space, students can always be enthused to ask questions. Following are some examples of questions that can be applied to engage the students:

- If you were in the scene, what would you see, hear, smell, feel?
- What do you think is happening outside of the picture?
- What was it like before?
- What do you think it will be like in the future?
- What 'geography' can you see in this picture?
- How do you think this was formed?

Video clips: A short video clip can be a fantastic device for engaging students. You may ask the students to brainstorm all the questions they have whilst they are watching the clip. You may choose to play a clip with the volume down, so that students have to interpret what is happening simply from the images from the scene. Or you may wish to flip this and play the audio only, and ask students to predict what the images on the screen would be. These strategies create a depth to thinking that can then be exploited to develop further questions related to the topic.

Stage 2: developing the enquiry questions

Once you have used your stimuli to engage the students and to get them thinking around your topic, those questions must be distilled down to a few key questions for the students to answer. The enquiry question or questions can be developed in two ways: either the students lead their own learning and create the question(s) for themselves, or the enquiry may require a certain amount of teacher influence to guide the students in the right direction. Both methods have their advantages and disadvantages.

Student-led enquiry

The enquiry question that the students wish to pursue may be the result of the stimuli you have already provided, or it may stem from their desire to discover their own answers. This desire may be the result of a class discussion at the start, middle or towards the end of the topic. To generate the enquiry question you may want to start by asking the following questions:

- What would you like to learn about during this topic?
- Which questions do you have about this topic so far?

- Which parts of the topic have you struggled with so far?
- Look back at your work. What would you still like to discover about this topic now that you have a better understanding of it?
- Look back at your previous test/feedback. What do you still need to learn or work on?

Having established the questions the students want to answer, students can be given the autonomy to find out the answers for themselves, or it may be necessary to support them in achieving their goal. The advantage of using this method is that it is totally student centred and reflective. Students are challenged to identify their own learning needs, which can help with motivation during the learning process. The disadvantage is that at this stage as the teacher you have little control of what the students are distinguishing as a learning need. This may greatly differ from your own thoughts or assessment. Therefore it may be necessary to intervene to jointly identify a need or a question to answer.

Teacher-led enquiry

In this instance the teacher is the driver of the enquiry. As the teacher you may have identified a learning need that can be approached through an enquiry process. You may select the particular question/hypothesis that you want the students to answer/investigate or you may offer a selection of differentiated questions to which the students must respond. Either way, there is a degree of control on the direction of the enquiry. Once you have set the questions, you may then provide the necessary resources for the students to use. You then control the activities and the content that the students use. The advantage for you as the teacher is that you can steer the support for students to the specific enquiry question identified. Also, this level of support may be necessary for lower attaining students who could struggle to focus on a particular area with such a wealth of information open to them. The disadvantage is that this method often leads to predictable conclusions, with little creativity generated by the students. Students may feel they have little say in which questions they would like to answer, taking away the autonomy we are striving to create.

Both student-led and teacher-led approaches have their merits. It is obvious that the best way to meet the needs of the students is through negotiation, discussing possible options and enquiry questions and allowing the students to choose; in this way they maintain autonomy whilst receiving directed support from the teacher when and where necessary. Table 7.1 lists possible question

Table 7.1 Differentiated question stems

Knowledge	• How would you explain . . . ? • Why . . . ? • When . . . ? • Where . . . ?
Comprehension	• How would you compare . . . ? • What evidence is there to support . . . ? • Which facts and ideas show . . . ? • What is the main idea of . . . ?
Application	• How would you show your understanding of . . . ? • What examples can you find to support . . . ? • Calculate . . . • How would you solve . . . ?
Analysis	• Why do you think . . . ? • What conclusions can you draw from . . . ? • What is the relationship between . . . ? • How would you classify . . . ?
Synthesis	• What would happen if . . . ? • Can you predict the outcome of . . . ? • How would you design . . . ? • Can you propose an alternative to . . . ?
Evaluation	• How would you prioritise . . . ? • Can you assess the value/importance . . . ? • Based on what you know how would you explain . . . ? • How would you evaluate . . . ?

stems that you may wish to use to support your students. They are based on Bloom's Taxonomy and thus they increase in the level of metacognition necessary to answer them.

Stage 3: success criteria

If the work that the students produce is to be assessed, then they need to work to success criteria. These act as the benchmark by which both you and the student will evaluate success. They offer clarity to your students as to what they need to do to achieve success in the enquiry. Table 7.2 provides example generic success criteria that can be used to support students.

You may choose to use a generic rubric or you may develop a rubric specific to a topic. This could be developed by the teacher or established through

Table 7.2 Success criteria for Enquiry Based Learning

Standard	Enquiry Question/ Hypothesis	Research	Presentation	Literacy	Numeracy
Mastery/Enhanced	I created my own research questions and selected the most appropriate one to investigate.	I used a range of research methods and information sources with confidence, including: textbooks, information technology (IT) and articles.	I used my research to write and produce my own work. I referenced all my work and was aware of bias from websites.	My spelling, punctuation and grammar are correct throughout.	All calculations are correct with workings out. Graphs and diagrams are accurately drawn and fully labelled using the correct axis and units.
Secure	I created my own research questions and, with help, chose the best one to investigate.	I used a limited range of research methods with guidance.	I produced my own work based upon my research.	Generally my spelling, punctuation, and grammar are correct throughout. I make slight errors with more difficult words and key terms.	Calculations are correct but not all working out is shown. Graphs are well drawn and labelled.
Developing	I had help to write and develop my research question.	I was guided as to which books and websites to use.	I created my presentation with some guidance and assistance.	I can spell commonly used words; however there are some mistakes within my work.	I was supported to complete calculations, and I needed guidance to draw graphs and diagrams accurately.

negotiation with the class, asking 'What do we think would make the best investigations?', 'What would the best investigations include?' or 'What does success look like?'

Stage 4: planning

Once the enquiry question has been designed, and after some discussion on what success looks like, it is time for the students to plan how they will go about answering their question. This may be directed by the teacher or you may wish to give the students increased independence by asking them how they will carry out their investigation. The final goal can often appear daunting to students, especially if you have modelled excellent previous projects by students to show them what you are expecting. The key is to stress to the students that Enquiry Based Learning is a process, and to break the project down into manageable chunks. It is then the incremental steps and improvements that will result in the desired outcome. I use the planning sheet shown in Figure 7.2 with my students so that they are able to think through and visualise the process.

The students are challenged to come up with initial ideas about how they will approach the enquiry. The questions on the sheet act as prompts to get the students to think more deeply about their enquiry prior to starting it. This stops students going off in the wrong direction or collecting data or information that is not relevant. It is not a requirement for students to complete all of the boxes; in fact they may only fill in the first three. This allows them to move through the process as they gain more knowledge and understanding. Students may need to add steps into the process to reach their desired outcome. The teacher's role will be to support students in the 'steps' process, clarifying what they need to research or discover, where they can find the information and discussing the reliability of the sources.

Stage 5: resource materials for research and challenge

This stage is when the students are able to engage with source material. As you may have offered the students a range of options for their enquiry, this can be potentially the hardest stage to manage. Ideally students take ownership of their own learning and become autonomous learners; however, to achieve this, a lot of support may be needed. Rather than simply telling the students where to find all the information they need, you can ask a series of coaching questions. These will still create the desired outcome, but the students will be required to think more deeply and develop more independence. Following are several questions that you could ask the students:

- 'Where do you think you could find the answer to your question?'
- 'How reliable do you think that source material will be?'
- 'Is your source material biased?'
- 'Have you prioritised your research?'

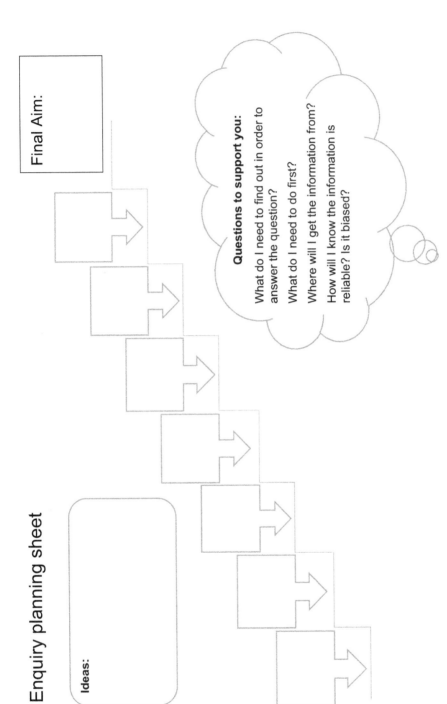

Enquiry planning sheet

Final Aim:

Ideas:

Questions to support you:

What do I need to find out in order to answer the question?

What do I need to do first?

Where will I get the information from?

How will I know the information is reliable? Is it biased?

Figure 7.2 Enquiry planning sheet

- 'What does success look like?'
- 'It that realistic?'
- 'What approaches have you used in similar situations?'
- 'What else could you do?'
- 'Who could you ask to help you?'
- 'Would you like me to offer you some suggestions?'
- 'Does this work answer your question?'
- 'What can I do to support you?'

If you model research skills and demonstrate how to navigate through abundant information on the Internet, then the students can quickly acquire the skills to become effective and efficient researchers.

The Internet will be the first source of information for most students. Demonstrate how to use search engines efficiently. I model the difference between typing in a vague term such as 'volcanoes' compared to searching on 'causes of the 1994 eruption of Mount Etna'. These call up vastly different websites to investigate. Getting students to craft concise and efficient search terms is the aim, but wasting time looking at irrelevant sites or links to other stories can be a major stumbling block. The key is to set strict parameters: you may want to state specific time boundaries within lessons; for example, 'You have 30 minutes in today's lessons to produce two A4 pages with three pictures.' The benefit of this instruction is that it creates a sense of urgency for the students, and also challenges them to prioritise their information, making them think 'Which are my three best pictures?' 'Do I need all this information or is a lot of it irrelevant'?

You may need to direct the students to source material. Table 7.3 shows a range of source materials that can be used.

How the students access this information is up to you. With the wealth of multimedia technology around today, students can access a plethora of information with a variety of options available to them. Smartphones, Apple iPads, laptops and Google Chromebooks are just a few of the possibilities, let alone a visit to the library or the use of textbooks. There are a number of advantages and disadvantages for each of the options, and it is your role to support the students as and when necessary to ensure they are on the right track.

Table 7.3 Sources of information for Enquiry Based Learning

Written	Images	Data	Maps	Others
Textbooks	Photographs/ field sketches	Government statistics	Street maps	Specimens (e.g. rocks)
Newspaper articles	Satellite images	Graphs	Google maps	Videos
Journals	Textbook	Tables	Ordnance Survey maps	Documentaries
Websites/Twitter	Diagrams	Choropleth maps	Atlases	YouTube
Letters/leaflets	Google maps	Desire lines	GIS	Radio programmes/clips
Official documents (e.g. government and Environment Agency reports)	Cartoons	Primary data collection	Maps from brochures/leaflets	Animations

Problems associated with research and resources

As mentioned previously, this stage can be the hardest to manage as the students have such autonomy. Students can often become frustrated when they cannot find the information they need, or their motivation may drop if they do not feel they are making progress.

Peer support can be a great tool to help students solve the problems between themselves: sharing good practice during a review session or pairing up students for a short time may be all that is required to get the students back on track. Using lead learners may go some way to solving any issues. However, the best way to prevent problems from arising is to provide students with ongoing progress feedback that they can easily understand and act upon. This progress feedback should concentrate on what they need to do to improve their work and offer steps on how to achieve this. Regular feedback serves two purposes: the first is to improve the academic achievement of the student and the second is to promote student motivation.

Independent learning is reliant upon intrinsic motivation, the student's desire to discover new knowledge and learn more about a given topic. Hopefully students have intrinsic motivation for this challenge since they have taken ownership and assumed control of their own learning, established their own learning goals, and are finding the motivation from within to progress towards success. However, as problems arise motivation can drop and ebb; the challenge is what can then be done to enthuse and inspire the students again. As mentioned earlier, feedback can be a major tool in achieving this.

Setting smaller, short-term goals within the lesson can help to make the larger task more manageable. Take students back to the planning stage: if this has been completed in detail, then students may just need a reminder of which step they are on, and a positive word on how well they have done so far. If this has not been completed to your satisfaction, now is the time to address the problem and revisit the steps necessary for success: use the prompt questions to get the student back on track and reengaged with the challenge.

Reminding the students about the purpose of their work can also be the key to reengagement. If students know and believe that there is a point to them working hard, then this can serve as the motivator.

Stage 6: methods of presentation

Once all the necessary research has been done and information has been gathered, the students will then need to present their findings. This can be achieved in a wide variety of ways. Again this may be the student's choice or you may wish to organise this yourself. Following are a number of ideas for students to present their work. Obviously there can be a combination of techniques.

Storyboards: these can be an effective method of presentation for smaller enquiries. The premise is that you combine a picture with a text caption. The number of pictures and captions can be determined by either you or the student. They are a good way to get students to link ideas together, as each frame should fit within the context of the 'story' they are trying to tell.

Learning logs: these are personalised learning resources created by the student. Within them are the various stages of the learning process, from the development of the initial learning question right through to the completed piece of work. They are useful for tracking progress and can be used to engage students with the learning process. Students can record all their rough work and notes as well as their final piece of work.

Movies: creating a movie can be an excellent hook for a number of students, because movies offer a visual representation of the learning question, combining images with text to explain processes, ideas or theories. The advantages are that movies tend to be highly motivational for many students, since they are a blend of images, text and music/commentary. They are also a great medium for students to work with, offering challenge and engagement. The disadvantages are, however, that they do require a certain amount of expertise and knowhow; therefore if you, as the teacher, are not competent with the technology, then you are reliant upon the students' own knowledge and you may struggle to support or challenge them. Another disadvantage is that students tend to get caught up selecting all the relevant images or video clips, and the knowledge and understanding including the text suffers as a result. Therefore this option may require more direct supervision or intervention.

Graphic organisers: these can provide a simple yet effective way of organising key ideas and synthesising work. There are many types of graphic organisers that can be used to present work. The advantage is that they will require students to evaluate which information is relevant, synthesise ideas and concepts, and then prioritise which information they choose to use.

Foldables: these useful devices, developed by Dinah Zike, require students to consolidate their learning. After students have learnt about a particular topic during the enquiry, I ask them to produce a foldable on that work. This can be as creative and colourful as possible. It involves students having to synthesise what they have been working on, prioritise what they consider to be most important and then organise information in a creative way. The information is displayed in a number of ways using folded paper or card. Students can research the different designs you can make out of card by searching on 'Dinah Zike foldables'. There are many designs that can be used. Foldables provide an effective way of consolidating learning and applying what the students have learnt in a different way. Use the paper or card to make booklets, standing displays or even, as I have done, ask the students to design and create their very own revision hats. All can be wonderful creations with all the important information stored on them.

Dioramas: students really enjoy making dioramas. Essentially a diorama is a model representing a scene. It may be the outcome after the students have carried out research for their enquiry. Once they have investigated a particular environment they can make their own model to represent the concept or idea. For example, students research 'What is it like in a hot desert?' Once the students have researched the location of the deserts and the climate of desert areas, as well as the adaptions of the flora and fauna, then they can produce their own desert scene. I use takeaway cartons for students to make 'biomes in a box'.

Another idea for dioramas is using A4 paper ream boxes and creating a scene within the box that can be viewed only through a peephole: for example, a rainforest scene. You can also use a box which on the outside is decorated with features on the Earth's surface, created by plate tectonics such as fold mountains and volcanoes; once you look inside the box there is a scene of the structure of the Earth, with convection currents, the mantle, and the outer and inner core.

Podcasts: creating a podcast may be more of an innovative way for students to present their enquiry. Podcasts can be relatively easy to create. Most laptops have voice recording software or students may use smartphones or tablets with voice recording apps. Having decided on the content, students will then need to produce a script or create cue cards to read from. If the students want to develop this further, they can edit their podcasts with free editing software available on the Internet, adding music and sound effects. They can upload the completed podcasts onto social media to share with classmates if they wish.

Animations: there are a number of free web tools for creating animated video presentations. Students can access very useful online tutorials to teach the students how they work. In a very short space of time, students can master the software, producing some fantastic presentations that allow them to develop their creativity and also subject knowledge. It is important to keep students on track when using such technology, as they can become fixated on the animation and not the geographical learning which is the most important aspect.

When discussing the methods of presentation with the students, it is important to challenge the students to try something new. Given the chance I assume that most students would opt to produce a Microsoft PowerPoint or a leaflet, because they are comfortable and confident with the technologies and the methods behind them. If we truly want to stretch and challenge our students we should aim to encourage them to work outside of their comfort zone. Yes, a PowerPoint would work fine – but is there another option that the students could use? For example, could they make a movie instead? Why not challenge them to make a diorama as well?

Stage 7: reflect/review

Students should be given the opportunity to reflect on and review their work. This requires the students to internalise what they have been learning about, and to think about which skills they have developed and what they now know and understand. I ask my students to record the following in their exercise books:

- Two skills they have developed
- Six key points they have learnt, in order of priority
- One 'What Went Well' during the topic

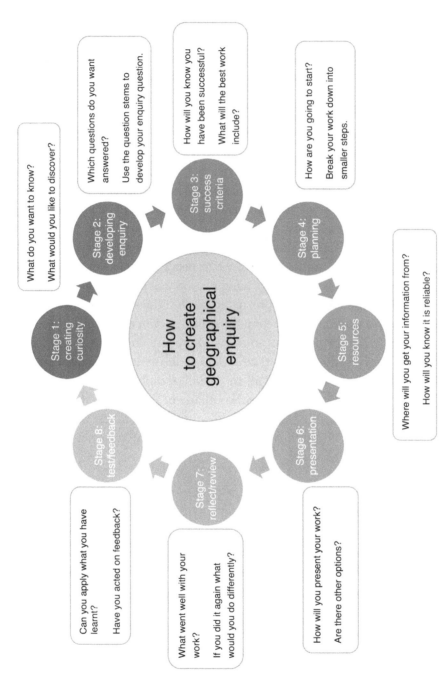

Figure 7.3 How to create geographical enquiry

- One 'Even Better If' statement
- One question they still have about the topic
- One target for next time we do an enquiry challenge

Stage 8: test/feedback

Once the students have completed their enquiry and reviewed their work, you may wish to take the opportunity to test/assess the students on which skills, knowledge and understanding they have developed, the principle being that they now apply what they have learnt. This assessment will then inform your future planning. Where are the gaps in knowledge? Which skills do they still need to develop? If you have shared the success criteria with the students prior to the enquiry then they should have a clearer picture of what they need to do to achieve success. The use of success criteria also makes it easier for you to mark the work, as you have a set of standards to mark against.

The feedback you give to the students can then be directly linked to the success criteria. The criteria set the benchmark for each level or expectation; therefore, in your feedback, you can directly quote from the rubric. Regardless of the final grade or score it is important to praise the progress. The enquiry process can be very challenging for students, so if they have been able to achieve and develop it is important to recognise this in the feedback. Figure 7.3, 'Enquiry geography in a nutshell' helps to condense the key aspects of this chapter.

> **Enquiry geography in a nutshell**
>
> - The power of Enquiry Based Learning is that it enhances engagement and fosters a deep understanding through a research-based approach.
> - It is important for students to develop their geographical understanding by making connections between their existing understanding and new knowledge.

Figure 7.4 Enquiry geography in a nutshell

CHAPTER 8

Literacy in geography

Whenever I start talking about literacy to a group of geography teachers I always see some staff in the audience switch off, and I can almost hear their collective groans. The reason for this response is that some teachers feel that literacy should be taught by the English department, and that as geography teachers they are too busy teaching the content of the course to worry about teaching a lesson on literacy. What they, of course, fail to realise is that the two strands are intertwined, and that their students' success in geography is dependent upon their success in literacy. This message should not come as a great shock to you. You don't have to start rewriting schemes of work or changing your lesson plans to include 'how to use an apostrophe'. The reality is that you are already using literacy in every lesson, and becoming outstanding is about recognising those opportunities to improve the student's skills. The point is that it's not about literacy: it's about outstanding teaching. If I am a teacher of geography, I have to take responsibility to teach my students how to read and write and speak like a geographer. That's not about literacy: it's about good teaching.

Whether the students are speaking, reading or writing there are always opportunities to improve, and with your guidance, support and teaching those same students can thrive and flourish in your lessons.

Geography has its own nuance of communication. The way in which geographers speak (the terminology and subject specific terms we use), read (the way we analyse text) and write (balanced) means that geography has a unique set of literacy standards. Even within our geography departments we have our own way of talking about our subject. We have developed our own language conventions and vocabulary. It's the process of sharing this with students, and teaching them the necessary literacy skills, that is so important for ensuring that they are successful in our subject. If we spend a little more time each lesson developing those communication skills, the sum of all the parts could have a considerable positive impact on student performance.

Literacy can be divided into three parts: speaking, reading and writing. Following are a number of ideas to enhance your teaching of communication within your lessons. As mentioned previously, it must be remembered that literacy does not need to be a discrete lesson, rather habitual everyday practice that maximises every opportunity to exploit the specific literacy skills.

Speaking: you set the standards

As the teacher you set the standards of oracy, so have high expectations. If you willingly accept one-word answers, then that becomes the norm and it is habit forming. There is a strong correlation between a student's verbal and writing ability, therefore if he/she is struggling to speak in a sentence then there will undoubtedly be a struggle to write a sentence. However, it is not purely about translating what students say onto their paper; it is more about developing a culture of learning dialogue within your classroom, so that students are able to discuss with both the teacher and their peers what they are learning and how they are learning it. The culture of talk can be created so that all students have the confidence to speak, ask questions, formulate answers and contribute during the lesson.

Ideas to encourage speaking and engagement within lessons

1   **Speak in sentences:** insist that students answer in full sentences. This one rule alone has had a considerable impact on the performance of my students. To begin with this can seem laborious and time consuming, constantly having to remind them to put their answer in a sentence, but they soon pick up the practice. Obviously there may be times when you want a quick, one-word response, but by maintaining a 'speak in sentences' rule you should quickly see the benefits. You may need to model the kind of language you are expecting or ask other students to support. Techniques such as Pose, Pause, Pounce, Bounce and others discussed in the Chapter 5, 'Questioning', can be used effectively to develop oracy and an understanding of what is expected.

2   **Give me an answer with the word . . . in:** this is an additional technique built on the 'speak in sentences' rule. It is a great way to get students to structure answers and improve their geographical vocabulary. Using key terminology, you can request that students use a particular word in their answer. You may wish to use impressive vocabulary so that the students

become familiar with the terms, thus gaining in confidence to use them themselves. Below are several examples:

Teacher: 'Give me an answer with the word **erosion** in it.'

Students: 'A wave cut platform is a landform created by **erosion.**'

Teacher: 'Give me an answer using the term **mitigate.**'

Students: 'There are several ways in which building designers can **mitigate** against the effects of an earthquake.'

Teacher: 'Give me an answer with the word **baobab** and **climate** in it.'

Student: The **baobab** tree has adapted to the savanna **climate** by having a deep tap root to search for water.'

3   **Speaking activities:** introduce speaking activities into your lesson. This should not be purely a novelty in order to tick a few boxes but rather an opportunity to develop. The concept is that the lesson involves a speaking activity, or a range of speaking activities, to promote communication skills. Following are a few suggestions for you to consider:

○   **Country presentations:** whilst studying Africa with Year 8, each student selects an African country out of a hat, and he/she has to research and produce a presentation based upon the chosen country. You can provide the necessary guidance on what the presentation should contain (e.g. physical and human landmarks, details of the capital city, food and culture etc.). Then the students are given the freedom to make their presentation in any format, the only rule being that they have to talk about their country. I appreciate that some students may struggle with this activity, in which case you could pair up students with lead learners.

○   **Barrier games:** this is a fun way to challenge your students whilst also improving their communication skills. Ask students to sit back to back and then one student has to describe what he/she can see in a picture, whilst the other student draws a picture based on the description. This could be a pre-prepared picture or pictures, or simply a picture from a particular page in a textbook. To enhance and add challenge to this activity, students could be asked to used subject specific terms or they could be banned from using certain words in their description. This can then be followed up with questions about the success of the activity. What went well? Which were the best descriptions? What made them so good? Which words did they use? To reduce your preparation time, ask students to collect pictures on a particular theme for you as homework.

These can then be used in the next lesson by collecting them in, mixing them up, and then redistributing or using them for another lesson.

○ **Grandma went to market:** you may remember this memory game as a child; it requires all students to participate and talk whilst also testing recall and building memory. It begins with 'Grandma went to market.' You then add an item – for example, she bought eggs – then the next student must repeat the items as well as adding another item to the list. You can then work your way around the class with each student contributing to the list. This can be adapted to our subject, so instead of 'grandma went to market' it can become:

- I went on a geography field trip to a river valley and I saw . . .
- The features of Birmingham's CBD are . . .
- Walking through the tropical rainforest I saw . . .

○ **Just a minute:** For this challenge students are given 1 minute to talk to their partner about a chosen topic. This could be what they learnt during the last lesson, what they already know about a particular subject or a picture displayed on the board. As students develop their communication skills, I introduce more conditions to the task. They have to talk for a minute without hesitation or repetition. Then they have to use a selection of keywords in their monologue. The challenges can become harder as they begin to master the skills. To involve the students who are passively listening I ask them to tally up the number of keywords their partner has used. Then they swap over. For me this represents 2 minutes of quality learning involving recall of information, knowledge of a particular topic, sufficient understanding to be able to explain to another student as well as the various literacy skills of speaking in sentences, using specialist terms and connectives.

○ **Speed dating:** For this activity students may need to arrange their desks so that they can move around the room and also sit opposite to one another. I find a horseshoe arrangement works best, with students sitting on the outside and inside of the desks, or you may clear away the desks and just have two circles of students. With students sitting opposite to each other they have 2 minutes to discuss what they have learnt during the lesson. Then once the time is up, I ask the inner circle of students to move around one place, so that everyone is now talking to someone else. This is a fantastic way to get students to talk about their learning – and in my experience, because the time allowed is so short, they are rarely off task. Depending on your class, you may want to shorten the time or lengthen it, but I find an online timer projected onto the board works well

To introduce an idea	To illustrate a point	To add a point	To sequence ideas	Conclusions	Impressive vocabulary
• Regarding • In my opinion • The evidence suggests • Firstly we must consider • Having considered	• As the research shows • For example • To demonstrate • As the evidence shows • The results indicate	• It must also be considered • Firstly, secondly • In addition to • Furthermore • Consequently	• More importantly • Not only that but • Subsequently • Initially • Following on from	• In conclusion • To sum up • To summarise • We can ascertain • Overall	• Plethora • Zenith • Circumspect • Cumulative • Appease • Superfluous • Complacent

Figure 8.1 Structuring formal talk

so the students can see how much time is remaining. If you feel the class may lack confidence in such an activity you can give the students time to produce learning resources that they can use when explaining what they have learnt. I always enjoy this challenge: it is a great way to see all students on task and actively engaging in discussions about geography.

○ **Make keywords explicit:** Whenever you or your students say a keyword, make reference to it. Whenever I hear a key term I draw attention to it by telling the class 'nice use of keywords' and then I write it on the board. Part of my board is sectioned off just for this purpose, so as the lesson progresses I can add to the list. This then supports the students with their work as they can see the words on the board, and it serves as a reminder to include the words in their work.

○ **Structuring formal talk:** To help establish formal talk and the use of standard English within lessons, use a literacy mat or prompt card to remind and support students of vocabulary they should be using. The example in Figure 8.1 can help students to increase and improve their vocabulary and, over time, this support can be withdrawn. Often when I teach a lesson which involves speaking activities such as a debate I ask students to create their own prompt cards for homework; the results are always impressive. Following on from this they can then create a number of prompts for a range of speaking activities including persuasive speeches, monologues, presentations or story-telling.

Reading: how to get students to engage with text and read effectively

Reading is key for knowledge acquisition; yet it feels at times that reading has become considered geeky, unfashionable and has lost its relevance in the classroom. If we, as teachers, don't hold it in high regard or accentuate its importance, then the students certainly won't. Geoff Barton likens the approach to reading to the Matthew Effect, which is based upon the parable of Matthew 13:12: the rich shall get richer whilst the poorer shall get poorer. Barton connects this to the idea that the word-rich shall get richer and the word-poor shall get poorer. This is developed further by Daniel Rigney: 'While good readers gain new skills very rapidly, and quickly move from learning to read to reading to learn, poor readers become increasingly frustrated with the act of reading, and try to avoid reading where possible' (2010: 76). Rigney recognised that 'Students who begin with high verbal aptitudes find themselves in verbally enriched social environments and have a double advantage' (2010: 76). This fact is supported by The Department for Education (DFE) research that states that by the age of 7, children in the top quartile have 7,100 words; children in the lowest have around 3,000. As students move through the education system this problem becomes exacerbated. Students are reluctant to read because they can't do it very well and thus they fall further and further behind, whilst those who can read and enjoy reading exponentially increase their knowledge and understanding.

Reciprocal reading

This is a practice widely used at primary schools, and having seen it used, I wonder why it is not more commonly integrated within the secondary classroom. It involves students actively engaging with text to improve their understanding and comprehension of both fiction and non-fiction. It involves four challenges for students to consider:

1   **Predict:** Having provided the students with relevant text, whether this is a textbook or worksheet, the students' challenge is to predict what they will be reading about and what will happen. If there are any visual cues on a page, they can use the cues to help them, as they attempt to predict what the text will include and discuss. Their prediction can be recorded in their exercise book or just discussed as a class. Students could use the following sentence stems:

   ○   I think this text is about . . .

   ○   I predict . . .

   ○   I think I will learn about . . .

   ○   I imagine . . .

   Students then read the text to discover if they are correct in their predictions. They could record the differences before and after if you wish. This activity may necessitate a certain amount of guidance from the teacher. For example, if the title of the chapter is 'The effects of volcanic eruptions' then the students have a fair chance of knowing the content; however if you ask the higher-level question 'What do you think the effects of a volcanic eruption are?' students will be required to consider more deeply what the text may include.

2   **Question:** As students read the text, you may ask them to engage with some or all of the following lower level question stems. Again, this involves students becoming active with the text rather than passively skim reading and not absorbing the information or making connections.

   ○   Who . . . ?
   ○   What . . . ?
   ○   When . . . ?
   ○   Where . . . ?
   ○   Why . . . ?
   ○   How . . . ?
   ○   Which . . . ?
   ○   What if . . . ?
   ○   How ought . . . ?
   ○   Describe . . .

3   **Clarify:** This challenge tests the comprehension skills of the students. Have they really understood what they have just read? You may need to prompt students to reread the text or try to connect to other concepts or ideas that they have been learning about. This is also an opportunity for students to record questions to clarify. As students read the text they may have questions which they want to ask to clarify their understanding of the topic, or they may be curious about a certain point – for example, 'Where exactly is Mount Etna?' These questions could be noted down in their exercise books or recorded on sticky notes that the students can then put on the board for the teacher/students to engage with later. You could ask the students to come to the board and select three questions that they then have to go away to research and answer, either in the lesson or as homework for the next lesson. Possible question stems for students follow; ask students to write down any questions that they may have about the text:

   ○   I didn't get . . .
   ○   What does . . . mean?

Predict	Before...	Question	
I think this is about ... I think I will learn...	After...	Who, What, When, Where, Why, How, What if ?	
Clarify	Words/ideas to clarify:	Summarise	
I didn't get...	How I clarified:	This is about... First...then...finally...	

Spellings _____ Definitions _____

_____

_____

Figure 8.2 Guided reading sheet

- I don't understand . . .
- Can you explain . . . ?

4 Summarise: This challenge requires higher-level thinking from students. They are asked to summarise and prioritise the text they have just read, dissecting the text and picking out the most important points. Then they can be asked to prioritise those points. As the teacher you may want to confine this activity to six key points from the text and then number them in order of priority. One subsidiary challenge may be to reduce the six key points to six keywords and then to one keyword to sum up the whole text. Figure 8.2 is an example of a guided reading sheet I use with my students.

Storyboards

This activity has been around for many years, but it is wonderful for getting students to select key points and visually represent the text. It also serves as a great way to revise. Students select the most relevant points and, depending upon what you want, they may write a caption underneath, or you may ask them to represent the text with pictures but without any words. Students can then be challenged to retell the story using the pictures as cues. This can be used in many situations, for the recalling of case studies or to explain a geographical process such as the formation of ox bow lakes or how fold mountains are formed.

Reading races

Skimming and scanning are two widely known approaches to speed reading texts; they allow students to read though a vast amount of text quickly and can be efficient and effective techniques to aid study. These techniques can be used in reading races. You could divide your class into groups and give them all the same text. At your desk you have a series of questions to give to each group of students. On the instruction 'On your marks, get set, go', students race to your desk to collect the first question related to the text. Once they have found the answer by employing the skimming and scanning techniques, they then write it down and race back to you to check if the answer is correct. You can then send them back to find the correct answer, to improve their answer or give them the next question. I normally produce ten questions to keep students engaged throughout, as they can soon become disheartened if they fall well behind the rest of the class. I also produce a mixture of long and short response questions, considering how long I want them sitting at their desks searching for answers. The element of competition always creates a vibrant classroom, with students desperately searching through text to find the answers. It's rare to find them so transfixed with text.

This is a fantastic technique to captivate a class. However it is important to realise that it is unlikely to support their deeper understanding or knowledge of a topic. It serves as a great way to engage a class, but the students may not necessarily understand what they are writing down. You will probably need to go over the key points again. I often do a repeat test of the questions as a plenary to see what students can recall, or to discover if they have lost the information already.

Skimming

When you skim read your eyes dart across the page, trying to ascertain the gist or overall ideas of the text. To help students to skim read, teach them the three steps to effective skimming:

1   Read the entire first paragraph. This often gives you the structure to the text to follow, for example in a geography text the first paragraph might

introduce the cause, effect and response to an earthquake; students can therefore predict that if they want to learn about how people responded to the earthquake, the information will be nearer the bottom of the text.

2   Read the first sentence of each new paragraph. In most cases this will provide the main ideas of the paragraph.

3   Read the final paragraph completely. This often serves as a summary to all that has been discussed in the text.

Scanning

This is the fastest method of speed reading but does not require that students understand anything within the text. It is very useful if students are trying to find specific details for example the names, dates or places. Again, there are three simple principles to follow:

1   Concentrate on the word, fact or detail you are searching for; it is likely to appear more clearly in the text.

2   Look for the words in bold or italics as these can help you as you search through the text.

3   Use your finger to run across the page under the line of writing. However, let your finger run slightly faster than your eyes. You will find that this drags your eyes across the page more quickly.

Twenty words a minute

Having read a piece of text, students are challenged to write down twenty words associated with it within a minute. They have to think rapidly to complete the task. In my experience they find this challenge both frustrating, if their list is incomplete, and very rewarding if they meet the deadline.

Live reading

This requires you to read to the class. As you read, students jot down thoughts, ideas or their emotions created from the text. You may want to stop at the end of each paragraph to ask the students to note something down for each paragraph. Thus rather than the students sitting passively, they are engaged and listening carefully to the teacher. I make this challenge very open, allowing them to draw, produce a time line or draw emojis to tell the story of the text.

Reading aloud

Take every opportunity to encourage students to participate in your lesson. Ask students to read from the textbook or a presentation rather than doing it yourself. I realise that some students may be reticent to read since they often feel embarrassed or shy when reading in front of others. However if you can create a culture of reading aloud every lesson, whether this is their own work from their exercise book, from the textbook or even as part of the starter activity, it will develop confidence and the acceptance of reading.

For those students who are particularly determined not to read, it is important not to ignore them. I engage them by asking them to read the first three sentences. Then once they have finished I may say "Well read – carry on" or "Fab, finish the paragraph, thank you," In most cases, having started reading, they will comply with my instruction, so each time I'm extending the amount they are reading. Also, stopping them after three sentences allows me to choose somebody else if they have made several mistakes, and I can see that they are not comfortable to carry on.

Popcorn

This technique connected to reading aloud involves the class reading the same text. Once you have selected a student to begin reading, they read for as long or as little as they like. Once a student shouts 'popcorn' the reading 'pops' to another reader that they choose. This reader then takes over from where the last reader finished. This challenge requires all the students to be concentrating and following the text, so that if they are selected they are able to continue without hesitation. I am aware of some teachers who let the students pick a forfeit if a student hasn't been following the reader – for example they have to read in a funny voice or an accent.

Text mystery

This technique has been around for a while, but it is great for engaging the students with close reading. Take a piece of text and mix it up. You may choose to simply cut up text or change text around using a word processor. The challenge is then for the students to piece it back together in an order. This stretches students, making them consider chronology of events, how text fits together and sequencing. They have to close read to understand and order the text, thus engaging with it at a higher level than if it were just a normal page of text. I have used this technique successfully with A Level essays. Students have to piece together the essay into the format they consider to be the most relevant to the question.

Reading groups

This involves groups of students reading in silence. What could be better? Groups are given the same text to read quietly. Having read, they then discuss what they have read and develop three questions based upon the text. There is an opportunity for you to give different groups different texts, and then group envoys move around the class to discuss the different texts and report back to their group.

Writing: how to improve students' written work

Writing is a fundamental skill necessary throughout our lives. Within the school environment, it is through writing that students present ideas and thoughts, and how they demonstrate what they know. Writing is the device by which those same students are examined and consequently graded/scored; therefore if our students are going to be successful they must develop the ability to write with clarity, purpose and depth.

Within geography, students are required to write for a variety of purposes. Aside from the daily writing in sentences, if we consider the GCSE and A Level courses students need to be able to write to meet the following requirements:

- GCSE short response questions 1–4 marks
- GCSE longer response questions 6–9 marks
- A Level short response questions 1–6 marks
- Extended responses 10–40 marks
- Fieldwork
- Note taking

The reality is that students will not be able to simply create wonderful analytical prose with perfect paragraphs and faultless use of geographical terminology. The skills they require will need to be developed over time, resulting from continual practice, astute feedback and learning from mistakes. Writing fantastic extended responses and essays is a craft: students need to learn the necessary protocols and conventions necessary to write like an outstanding geographer.

F.A.I.L.: First Attempt In Learning

When asking students to write a piece of work, consider using the F.A.I.L. and S.A.I.L. approach. The phrase F.A.I.L. meaning First Attempt In Learning is attributed to the former president of India, Abdul Kalam; it means that you haven't failed at something, it was merely your first attempt in learning something new. Therefore S.A.I.L. represents Second Attempt In Learning. Applying this strategy has had one of the most positive impacts on my teaching practice in recent years.

When I first thought about introducing this strategy to my students I thought they would hate the idea, and be very reluctant to redraft work to have a second attempt at the same question. On the contrary, they love it. In fact they ask for more opportunities to try it in lessons. When I asked the students why they liked F.A.I.L. and S.A.I.L. lessons the overwhelming response was because they could see the improvement in their work so clearly between the two attempts. The clear improvement made them feel that they were making rapid progress, and their self-esteem soared. It is the rush of dopamine that students get once they feel they have achieved something that can become addictive, and thus they enjoy the lessons because they get the same rush every time.

It works in the following way:

1   Students are given a question to answer. This could be from a GCSE/A Level past paper or one you have created yourself. It is better if it requires an extended response as students can see the improvement more easily than in a shorter low-mark question.

2   Before students answer the question, stress to them that this will be their First Attempt In Learning and therefore they should give it a go, write what they think is necessary to answer the question and not to be afraid to make mistakes. This point cannot be over emphasised. The whole point of F.A.I.L. is that the students feel comfortable failing. The aim is to create a culture in the classroom that failing is a good thing because we learn from it, so we are able to improve. It is also important to note that no support should be given to the students: you do not need to provide writing frames or a list of keywords. This support will come later if necessary. Just encourage them all to write something; telling them to guess is a good way to engage those students who say 'I don't know.'

3   Once the students have completed their F.A.I.L. you can begin to unpick their work. I use a visualiser to showcase a student's work for the class to look at; we then unpick what is good and what could have been added to

improve the work. I appreciate that in the early stages you may not have an environment where students would feel comfortable sharing or commenting on others' work, yet this is something that can be quickly developed. At this stage you may need to dissect the actual question: for example, what are the command words? What do the keywords mean in the question?

4　Having a class discussion, where students share their ideas and good practice, is a wonderful way to develop the students' answers. They learn from each other, and thus appreciate the content or skills that they may need to improve in order to craft a better answer.

5　After sharing ideas and good practice, students begin their Second Attempt In Learning. You may have provided some structure at this point. You may have given them guidance on what to include in each paragraph, and you may have a list of key terms on the board that the students should include to improve their answer. You may have also modelled what a 'good' answer looks like or what a 'good' answer would include.

6　When the students have completed their work you may provide them with a mark scheme for them to mark their own work for the F.A.I.L. and S.A.I.L., or you may just show them where the marks were allocated for the answer. For the most impact, mark their work yourself for both their F.A.I.L. and S.A.I.L. This is where the progress is most evident. You will be able to clearly see the improvement made by the students. More importantly the students will see the improvement that they have made between the two attempts.

It is the improvement that the students make that shows this to be such a powerful technique. They can clearly see how, by following your instruction and guidance, they can improve their work, in some cases considerably.

Creating a culture of F.A.I.L.

The way you create a culture of acceptance of failure is vitally important to the success of F.A.I.L. It is important to take the time to talk to your class about the rationale behind F.A.I.L. lessons. I start by explaining that through failure we learn. I tell a story about how, when they start to learn to drive, they will be grinding gears, stalling, hitting the curb and leap frogging down the road. However this is highly unlikely to stop them ever getting behind the wheel again. They have a desire to pass their test and so they will keep on going, practising, learning, failing, learning and practising some more, until they pass. Then they will drive so much that the actions will become automatic: they will not have to think about putting their foot down to engage the clutch, to select the gear, to find the biting point before moving off. They will become unconsciously competent at driving.

It is this level of automaticity that we strive for our students to have when faced with extended writing tasks. They will not have to spend ages having to think about how to craft answers and how to write in paragraphs; they will do it almost automatically. Deconstructing the question, defining keywords, linking ideas, writing in paragraphs, using connectives – all this becomes automatic.

To help to promote the F.A.I.L. concept I have a number of posters in my room linked to failure and growth mindset. These include quotes from 'famous failures', for example:

> 'Failure is simply an opportunity to begin again, this time more intelligently.'
>
> – Henry Ford

> 'I have not failed, I have just found 10,000 ways that won't work.'
> – Thomas Edison on the invention of the light bulb

> 'I can accept failure, everyone fails at something, but I can't accept not trying.'
>
> – Michael Jordan

> 'It is impossible to live without failing at something, unless you live so cautiously that you might as well not have lived at all, in which case you have failed by default.'
>
> – J. K. Rowling

> 'You have to be able to accept failure to get better.'
>
> – LeBron James

In addition to the quotation posters I have a number of displays showing the F.A.I.L. acronym. All this serves to make failure and mistakes acceptable rather than students being unwilling to take risks through fear.

How you communicate and deal with failure and mistakes – both the students' and your own, is very important to the classroom culture. If you can create a culture that normalises errors, values the lessons learnt from them and makes 'struggle' an inevitable step to learning, then you can empower students to take risks without fear of ridicule or reprisal.

Ten techniques to improve your students' written work

1 **Structure support:** When a student is faced with an extended response question, for an outstanding answer from the student there needs to be a degree of structure. This therefore involves writing in paragraphs whenever the student writes about a new idea. A reminder of structure may be all your class needs to then progress with the challenge, or you may need to give additional support to your students. This is where your differentiation will be applied. For those requiring additional support you may want to question them on what they think needs to go into each paragraph, to help them to structure their work before they start. You could provide sentence stems to start them thinking or even model an answer. Figure 8.3 is an example of a support sheet that I used for an assessment. A powerful technique is to type or write the opening to an answer in front of the students, with the students. I ask them, 'How could we start this answer off?' Then we craft an answer together. This can be a messy process, with me deleting and rewriting new ideas from students, but that is the point. I demonstrate how it can be a messy process, sharing the idea that writing can be messy to begin with – frustrating in the middle – and glorious at the end.

2 **Connectives and keywords:** When I ask my students to complete a piece of writing I will often provide them with a literacy mat. This has lists of keywords and connectives to help students to link ideas and thus improve their work. Prior to them starting to write we will, as a class, have created a list of keywords that we think could be included into our answer to enhance the work and demonstrate our knowledge and understanding of the topic. I then challenge the students to use as many of the connectives and keywords in their work as possible. I give out two different coloured highlighters and the students develop their own key, one colour for connectives and one for keywords. Then, as they proofread their work they highlight all the connectives and keywords that they have used. The student who uses the most wins a prize.

3 **Literacy targets:** You may want to highlight the importance of certain literary devices by making specific targets for the students to work towards and achieve. This may be a generic class target or a personalised target for the students to note down in their book when you are marking. Table 8.1 shows some of the targets I use within my lessons.

4 **Modelling:** If you want students to be successful, show them what success looks like. I have a number of display boards around my room, showcasing

99

Literacy in geography

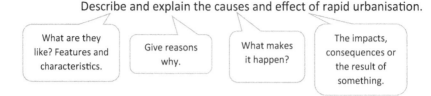

Describe and explain the causes and effect of rapid urbanisation.

> What are they like? Features and characteristics.

> Give reasons why.

> What makes it happen?

> The impacts, consequences or the result of something.

Paragraph 1: What is urbanisation? Give the definition of urbanisation and the two reasons for it.

- Rural to urban migration
- Natural increase

Paragraph 2: What are the reasons for rural to urban migration? Include push factors (reasons to leave the countryside) and pull factors (the attractions of the city). Explain what a natural increase is and how it can occur.

Paragraph 3: Problems of urbanisation: prioritise them and pick the main three to write about.

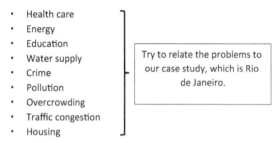

- Health care
- Energy
- Education
- Water supply
- Crime
- Pollution
- Overcrowding
- Traffic congestion
- Housing

> Try to relate the problems to our case study, which is Rio de Janeiro.

Paragraph 4: What are the problems and opportunities of squatter settlements (favelas)? Use facts and figures to support your answer. Think about different groups of people.

Paragraph 5: Conclusion. What do you think the future will be like for Rio de Janeiro? Is the current situation sustainable? What could be done to improve the lives of the residents?

Key words

- Urbanisation
- Migration
- Push and pull factors
- Pollution (atmospheric, visual, water)
- Rural
- Urban

- Favelas
- Inequality
- Infant mortality
- Megacity
- Sustainable
- Self-help scheme

Figure 8.3 Extended writing support sheet

good practice, that I can pull off the wall and distribute around the class. Each board illustrates a good example of different styles of written work. I have boards for writing to explain and writing to persuade, and a board to show how to interpret graphs. These boards can save time and save me from having to repeat myself. I simply stick them up at the front of the class

Table 8.1 Literacy targets

Literacy target	Target	How to achieve your target
LT1	Structure your work by writing in paragraphs.	Remember the TIPTOP rule. Start a new paragraph when you change Time, Place, Topic or Person.
		Plan out your answer first.
LT2	Link ideas together by using connectives.	Use your connective mat to help you link ideas together and to develop the point you are trying to make: so, because, although, despite, in addition.
LT3	Use impressive vocabulary throughout your work.	Use the thesaurus to come up with alternative words.
LT4	Use keywords in your writing.	Use the keywords on the board or on the wall in your writing.
LT5	Use full stops and capital letters consistently.	Remember every sentence starts with a capital letter. Every sentence finishes with a .?!
		Proper nouns need a capital letter: these include people and places.
LT6	Check your spelling.	Use the dictionary or word mats to check you are spelling correctly. Sound the word out in your head – this may help.
LT7	Proofread your work.	Closely read your work to check it makes sense and to spot any errors. Read using a pencil under each word to really make sure you are checking.
LT8	Read your questions carefully so you fully understand what you are being asked to do.	Highlight keywords or command words. Use the dictionary and thesaurus to check you understand the meanings of words or to look for similar words.
LT9	Use a range of sentences.	Use short sentences at the start of a paragraph. Use a mix of simple, compound and complex sentences.
LT10	Check your punctuation.	Remember that every sentence must finish with either a .?! Use apostrophes for possession or to replace a letter:
		• The boy's football (possession)
		• They're (replacement for they are)

and tell students that, if they are unsure or need to check that they are on track, they should come and look at the example board.

5 **Sentence design:** To improve the literary ability of students and to engage the reader, students should be encouraged to use a range of different sentences, not only short and long but also simple, compound and complex. Referring to these sentence styles within your lesson will help students transfer their knowledge between subjects.

○ Simple sentences: these contain a subject and a verb. Example: the river is deep.

○ Compound sentences: These join two simple sentences together. Example: the river is deep and wide.

○ Complex sentences: A complex sentence contains a conjunction such as, since, because, although. Example: the river is deep and wide because of the erosion that has taken place.

6 **Developing vocabulary:** This technique can be used when introducing specialist terms within the topic. I find it works best with the more technical words because the activity requires deeper thinking from the students. It can also be used as a homework activity to improve students' understanding of key terms. Students can complete the template shown in Figure 8.4 to develop their subject-specific vocabulary.

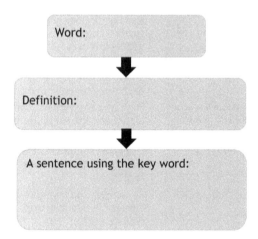

Figure 8.4 Developing vocabulary template

7 **Spelling:** Spelling is a significant feature of successful writing and communication. We can support our students by teaching them spelling strategies. These strategies can be divided into three approaches.

a Sounds: how does the word sound? Sound it out with them. Each subject will have common words that are frequently misspelt, so one approach is to sound those words out with them. This can be linked to the next approach, visual cues. Write them on the board phonetically: en-vi-ron-ment, gov-ern-ment.

b   Visual: show them what the word looks like. Break it down and sound it out: tem-per-a-ture.

c   Mnemonics: These can be very useful for commonly misspelt words such as 'necessary' (Never eat cakes eat salmon sandwiches and remain young) and 'because' (Big elephants can always understand small elephants). I have several of the more common subject specific words displayed around the classroom, with a number of mnemonics to help remember how to spell them correctly.

8   **Writing talk:** Give students the opportunity to discuss what they are going to write. This could be a group activity or within pairs. The chance to orally rehearse what they are about to write allows the students thinking time so they can consider their answer before putting pen to paper.

9   **Writing time:** If you want outstanding written work then you must give the students adequate time to produce it. When the students are first developing their skills it is important to give them the opportunity to finish their written work to their satisfaction, so they feel that they have accomplished their challenge. Then, as they develop, you may introduce more time constraints to prepare them to be able to write under the time limits of an examination. During exam practice lessons I ask the students to work under exam conditions where I instruct them to work on the basis of a mark a minute: thus for a six-mark question I give the students 6 minutes to answer.

10 **Spelling test:** With the increased importance of the Spelling, Punctuation and Grammar category I feel it is necessary to address the spelling ability of my students. This is best achieved with a spelling test. I run this on the F.A.I.L. and S.A.I.L. model so that students can see how they have improved over time.

At the beginning of a topic, without warning, I give the students a ten-word spelling test on the keywords. This serves as their F.A.I.L. Once the tests are completed, I go through the correct spellings with students, who write out three times any mistakes they have made. After several weeks we revisit the test, with the students having to spell the same words. This becomes the S.A.I.L. Having finished, students refer back to their original test to calculate any improvement. I then ask the students to record this as follows:

■   I have improved my score by . . . I am still misspelling . . .

■   I have reduced my score by . . . I am still misspelling . . .

If students were absent for the first test, you could test them again or ask them to test themselves in the future. Figure 8.5 is a summary of the chapter and acts as a reminder of this key area.

Literacy in a nutshell

- If you want outstanding geographers then you must teach them how to speak, read and write like outstanding geographers.
- Speaking: You set the standards within your classroom, don't accept one word answers and only accept formal language.
- Reading: Develop active reading skills by asking the students to predict, question, clarify and summarise text.
- Ask students to read aloud rather than you.
- Writing: Writing is a process that is often messy to begin with, frustrating in the middle and glorious at the end.
- Give time for students to practise writing with F.A.I.L and S.A.I.L lessons.
- Get students to plan and structure their written work before they start writing.
- Set literacy targets for the students.

Figure 8.5 Literacy in a nutshell

CHAPTER 9

Numeracy in geography

The ability to draw, interpret and analyse graphs, maps, tables and charts has always been a mainstay of geography. Now there is a plethora of other numerical skills necessary to master in the modern GCSE and A Level specifications. It is not merely the ability of students to become more numerically literate which is the only challenge for students and teachers; it is the application of these skills that is so vital to improve the student's geographical understanding and thus their progress with the subject. The key to improving students' numerical skills is through seizing the opportunity presented through our everyday teaching to incorporate and develop those skills. This does not imply that we should necessarily 'shoehorn' in specific lessons – however, this may be one approach that will successfully upskill our students. We should also acknowledge that numeracy in geography is not just primarily involved in skill development: we are also interested in developing the students' mathematical understanding and how this can be applied to the real world. In reality, when we discuss numeracy in geography we are essentially discussing mathematical thinking – not just the use of numbers, but more how the use of maths can help us improve our understanding of how the world works.

Dealing with data

Regardless of what type of graph, table or map you are asking the students to produce, I would always suggest scaffolding and modelling what you are after first. Then after practise and discussion the support can be withdrawn and the students can be given the opportunity to create the graphs, tables or maps for themselves. The level of support and scaffolding will depend upon the individuals in your class but it must be remembered that the end outcome is for all students to have the skill, knowledge and confidence to be able to work independently.

Constructing graphs, maps and tables

I will use the construction of climate graphs as an example yet the same ideas apply regardless of the graph, chart or table.

Before you even start the lesson consider the barriers you may face. Do the students have the correct equipment? Will all the students turn up with pens, pencils, rulers, calculators? How will you manage this if they do not? I have prepared a box of pens, pencils, rulers and calculators ready to distribute as necessary to avoid students being off task, which may then escalate to mis-behaviour. Do you need to reconsider your seating plan? Are there students you know of who can work together to support each other? Can high-attaining students work with low-attaining students to support them? Can you sit low-attaining students together so you can work with them on a separate table?

Once the logistics of the lesson are sorted out I begin by modelling how to construct a climate graph with the use of a visualiser. It projects onto the board the blank graph paper so students can see me construct the graph whilst I provide a running commentary, highlighting the necessary steps to completing the graph. Having provided the students with the data set I question them on the axis. What could go along the bottom of the graph? What could go up the sides? What scale could I use? Once we have established the axis I then begin to plot the data whilst asking the students any relevant questions. Having plotted data for the first three months, I then ask the students to draw and complete their own graph. I have a prepared support sheet to give out when necessary whilst also displaying the model graph on the board so students can see the axis. I use the same approach for any graph, table, chart or map I ask the students to produce. This demonstration and support is then withdrawn over time as and when necessary to meet the needs of the individual students. In time I will not use the visualiser and will just rely on the support sheet. Figure 9.1 is an example of a support sheet that can be distributed to the students. I can use the support sheet in two ways:

1 Distribute to the high-attaining students and instruct them to get on with their graph construction whilst I work with the low-attaining students.

2 Distribute to the low-attaining students and support them whilst the high-attaining students are challenged to recall the skills necessary without any support.

The allocation and subsequent discussion of the support sheet shows obvious progression with their skills as they develop them over time.

Student are then encouraged to check and peer-check their work. Is all the data plotted correctly? Was an appropriate scale used? Does the graph have a title? Are the axes labelled?

Step 1: Begin by drawing your axis, with the months along the bottom. Then you will need to think about your scale for both the temperature and the rainfall. What are your highest figures? How can this be divided equally on your scale? In this example two small squares equals one °c.

Month	J	F	M
Temperature	33	33	32
Rainfall mm	250	230	260

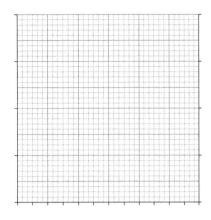

Step 2: Add the numbers and labels to the axis. Check that you have done this correctly. Don't forget to label the axis:

- Temperature °c
- Rainfall mm
- Months
- Title for the graph

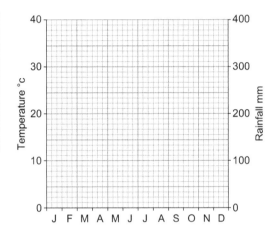

Step 3: Using the data plot the temperature line first. As you can see in the example the temperature for January was 33 °c. Use the left axis to plot the temperature.

Next plot the rainfall. Remember to use the right side axis! Look along the graph and then plot the figure for January. In this example it was 250 mm.

Once you have plotted all the figures, draw a smooth curve to connect the temperature points and colour in the rainfall bars.

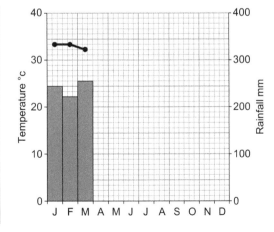

Figure 9.1 How to draw climate graphs

Data interpretation of graphs, maps and tables

Once the students have constructed their graph they are then challenged to 'use' the graph and data. This can involve a series of questions using command words. Describe, explain, analyse, interpret and justify can all be used as question stems depending upon the data in question. For a climate graph I may ask the following questions and use the supporting sentence stems shown underneath the question if necessary.

1   Describe the climate graph.

- ○   The maximum temperature was . . . the minimum temperature was . . . this is a range of . . .
- ○   The maximum rainfall was . . . the minimum rainfall was . . . this is a range of . . .
- ○   The pattern for the temperature was . . .
- ○   The pattern for the rainfall was . . .
- ○   There was an anomaly . . .

2   Interpret the climate graph.

- ○   The climate graph shows that . . .
- ○   The reasons for this are . . .

3   Justify why you chose that method of presentation.

- ○   Positives are . . .
- ○   Negatives are . . .
- ○   Limitation . . .

Regardless of what the graph, table or chart shows I try to encourage the students to use the following acronym (FRAP) where necessary and appropriate. I emphasise that it does not matter what the graph is about, the same acronym can be applied.

F: Figures. Use figures to support your answer. Manipulate the data rather than just lifting it off the page. Calculate the range, the percentage, the ratio.

R: Rate of change. Comment on the rate of change shown in the graph using phrases such as 'slow', 'rapid' and 'exponential'.

A: Anomalies. Are there anomalies in the data? What doesn't fit the pattern? What is the reason for this?

P: Pattern. What is the overall pattern? Is it increasing, decreasing or remaining constant?

If students apply the acronym FRAP then this gives a good foundation for their data interpretation. I begin by asking the students to recognise the pattern first, then back this up with figures to support the answer. It may then be appropriate to use more figures to describe the rate of change seen in the graph or to describe any anomalies. FRAP provides the foundation yet it does not explain the data. It is so important to spend some time investigating the data set rather than just seeing the completed graph as the end product. The graph should be seen as a stepping stone and just part of the process to answering the bigger question of 'why'. This is where the geographical thinking and understanding need to be applied. If we take the example of the climate graph, why is it that temperature and rainfall totals rise and fall? What is the reason for this? This can then lead on to subsequent learning about the movement of the sun, the movement of the intertropical convergence zone and the reasons for the seasons. This then helps the students to join up their thinking from a graph to their own experiences with the world around them and explain why they are wearing a coat in winter and why they are hot in summer, for example.

A useful system I use is for students to have a F.A.I.L. to interpret the graph (see Chapter 8 for a discussion of F.A.I.L. and S.A.I.L.). I pose an exam-style question and the students answer to the best of their ability. Then we discuss their first attempt and discuss how we could incorporate FRAP into the answer. Students then have their S.A.I.L. where they rewrite their answer. Once they have completed their answer they can then highlight where they have commented on the pattern, used figures to back up their answer, manipulated the data, identified anomalies and mentioned the rate of change. Both you and they should see a distinct improvement in their work.

When interpreting data, students may also be required to recognise or consider any bias in the data they are using. This can be an important consideration when questioning the validity of data. You will probably be aware of the saying 'you can prove anything with statistics' and thus all data must be questioned. For example data on climate change may be very different when sourced from environmental groups compared to from large oil companies. Ask the students what they would predict the data to show. Why might organisations want to use only specific data sets? There are a number of questions that can be used around the validity of data and the main aim is to get students to question if the data are reliable.

When constructing and interpreting data it is useful to remind the students that they need to transfer the skills they have developed in mathematics across to geography. Students sometimes fail to see the overlap between the subjects. They may be perfectly competent at calculating percentages in maths lessons yet appear to forget the basics when in the geography classroom. It is worth considering liaising with the maths department to establish what skills, knowledge and understanding the students should display in a given year group. There may even be opportunity to establish cross curricular links within the departments. Could instructors in the maths department use your primary data from a river investigation in their lessons? Could maths use development indicators to produce and interpret divided bar charts, for example?

As discussed in Chapter 2, geographical skills can be mapped and incorporated across the key stages to help to develop those specific skills. Table 9.1 shows the skills used in geography divided into three key sections: cartographic, graphical and statistical skills. I would suggest that where appropriate in your schemes of work and lesson planning you dedicate some time to the development of these skills and to the mathematical thinking surrounding them. The more you can acclimatise the students to the construction, interpretation and use of data the more numerically literate they will become, and this can be applied to their work to improve their performance. A summary of the key points from this chapter can be found in Figure 9.2.

Table 9.1 Numeracy skills in geography

Cartographic skills	
Latitude and longitude	Latitude and longitude are both measured in degrees. They are often used as coordinates to locate a specific place and site.
Maps	• Four- and six-figure grid references • Use of scale including 1:50,000 and 1:25,000 • Measuring distances, both straight and curved line • Use and understanding of gradient, contours and spot height • Use of compass directions • Identifying and describing landscape and relief • Identification of relief related to cross sectional drawings • Interpretation of cross sections and transects • Drawing inference of the physical and human landscape by the interpretation of map evidence including: patterns of relief, drainage, settlement, communication and land use

Graphical skills	
Construction and interpretation of graphs and diagrams	• Bar graphs, divided bar graphs, compound bar graphs • Histograms • Pictograms • Pie charts • Scattergraphs • Population pyramids/climate graphs • Choropleth maps • Isolines maps • Dot maps • Desire line maps • Flow line maps • Proportional symbols • Triangulation graphs
Statistical skills	
Measuring central tendency	• Mean, mode, median
Measuring dispersion	• Interquartile range • Standard deviation
Correlation testing	• Spearman's rank • Application of the significance level
Higher level tests	• Chi square • Mann Whitney U test

Numeracy in a nutshell

- Look for opportunities for students to engage with data, graphs and maps to improve their numerical literacy.
- Improve mathematical thinking by asking students to consider the outcomes of data sets and the reliability of data.
- Reherse students using the acronym F.R.A.P and allow them to practise this in lessons.
- Map and develop numeracy skills throughout the key stages.

Figure 9.2 Numeracy in a nutshell

CHAPTER 10

Geography in the news

One of the major attractions of studying geography is the fact that it is always current, ever changing and related to our lives. That is why it is so important to reflect this in our lessons.

When tragic natural disasters happen such as an earthquake this is an opportunity to enhance the students' understanding of the world around them, linking their learning to real-life situations and scenarios. Only through education and study can we ever hope to fully understand the processes that create such events and through this understanding we can aim to put in place strategies and procedures to help mitigate against such hazards.

Obviously not all geography in the news is linked to a natural disaster yet volcanic eruption, earthquakes, flooding, tropical storms, wildfires, drought and extreme weather events are all unfortunately commonplace throughout the year. Thus we should take every opportunity to educate our students about the world around them and current affairs.

Geography in the news can serve to meet a number of aims of the geography we teach in the classroom. It covers various scales – local, regional, national, international and global – and it covers all types of geographies including political, economic, physical, human and environmental geography. Table 10.1 demonstrates a few examples of real or potential news stories and how they can be related to geography.

Table 10.1 Geography in the news

Theme	News story example	Type of geography	Scale
Transport planning	The construction of a new local road The construction of a new runway at Heathrow The construction of HS2	Human, economic, political, environmental.	Local, regional, national, international

Theme	News story example	Type of geography	Scale
Volcanic eruption	The eruption of Mount Etna	Physical	International
Oil spill	Oil spill in the Gulf of Mexico	Environmental, political, human, economic	International, global
Fracking	Fracking companies being issued drilling licenses in the north of England	Environmental, political, human, economic, physical	Local, regional, national
Climate change: hottest summer on record	Peak temperatures reached around the country	Environmental, political, human, economic, physical	Local, national, global

Such stories as those in Table 10.1 can then be exploited to teach your students. I believe that using geography in the news helps to develop the case of just how important the study of geography is. It is the most current and contemporary subject on the curriculum since it is ever evolving and changing as the world evolves and changes too.

Strategies to utilise geography in the news

Marketplace

This idea from Paul Ginnis (2002) has been developed further by Jenny Britcliffe and incorporates many key principles for outstanding teaching. It involves a high degree of challenge and deep thinking as well as differentiated resources to support all learners. Students develop the literacy skills of reading, writing and oracy as well as the softer skills involved in teamwork. The activity can be used to develop an understanding of a current event. With creativity you can use that event to answer an extended response exam style question. This helps to develop knowledge and understanding of a case study and can be used effectively when geography is in the news. For this example students were given the learning question:

> 'Assess the primary and secondary effects and the responses to an earthquake event.'

For this activity students are divided into groups of four, and grouped based upon their ability or previous attainment scores. Grouping students on ability may be a crude way of selection, but you can use your professional discretion as to who sits with whom. The aim is for students to work with others of similar ability or attainment at this stage. Students then sit around a double table and either you or they number the students 1–4. This represents the 'home team'. For this example I will use a class of 24 students to demonstrate. (The layout of the desks and groups shown in Figure 10.1 is just an example. Students can be sat anywhere in the room as long as the students of similar abilities are sat together.)

High ability		Low ability		Middle ability		Low ability	
1	2	1	2	1	2	1	2
3	4	3	4	3	4	3	4

Middle ability		High ability	
1	2	1	2
3	4	3	4

Figure 10.1 Home teams

Once students are sat in their home teams, the first challenge is to dissect the exam question. Students identify the command word and the focus of the question. This is discussed as a class so all students are clear about what information they will need in order to be able to answer the question successfully.

Once the students have been numbered, they then move to work in their respective 'expert teams'. In this example there will be six students in each group, so they could be divided into two groups of three or all number 1s could work together (see Figure 10.2 for an example seating chart).

Mixed ability		Mixed ability		Mixed ability		Mixed ability	
1		2		3		4	
1	1	2	2	3	3	4	4

Mixed ability		Mixed ability		Mixed ability		Mixed ability	
1		2		3		4	
1	1	2	2	3	3	4	4

Figure 10.2 Expert teams

Once the students are sat in the respective expert teams, they are provided with the relevant resources to match their aspect of the question. The exam question can be divided into four relevant sections:

1 Location and background
2 Primary effects
3 Secondary effects
4 Responses

In this example, Expert Team 1 will receive the resources for 'location and background', Expert Team 2 will be given 'primary effect', and so on. The challenge is then to convert the text into a series of images and pictures that the students can then return to their home teams and teach the others in their group. To do this, members of the expert teams can support and help each other to develop their teaching resources on their given theme. The students are allowed to write down some key statistics and words but the aim is to generate pictures. This is because you want the students to teach each other when they return to their home team rather than just write down some key points for the other students in their group to simply copy. The point of this activity is to get the students to teach each other, which requires a deeper level of understanding. Once the students have developed their teaching resources and discussed the resource in their expert team, they then return to their home team.

Once back in their home team, students then go round the group in order, with number 1s going first to teach the others about their aspect of the question. The other students then have the opportunity to make notes from the mini lesson on their record sheet (see Figure 10.3). Once they have completed the mini lesson the others in the group can ask questions to clarify their understanding.

Location and background (plates involved, magnitude)	Primary effect (immediate effects)
Secondary effects (those effects that have come later after the initial event)	Response (how the government, aid agencies and local services responded)

Figure 10.3 Geography in the news record sheet

Once every student in the group has spoken, then the students can begin to write their answer to the exam question, with each section of the record sheet representing a different paragraph of their written answer.

Graffiti wall

For this challenge students are asked to bring in their own research on a particular news story. Then prior to the students entering the class I would have set up my graffiti wall. This may be a display board or I use the back of old wallpaper pinned to the wall. Students are then given board markers or felt tip pens then write down what information they have gathered. Depending upon the news story, you may choose to divide the paper up into sections. For example, for a flood event you may section the paper up into causes, primary effects, secondary effect, responses and solutions. Obviously this is dependent upon the timescale of the event. If the flood occurred only yesterday there will be limited information on responses, for example. However, you may wish to bring in another layer of challenge by asking the students to predict what will happen. What will the secondary effects be? How should the government, local services and public respond? What do you think the solutions are to the problem? This added challenge can create deeper thinking to the issue.

To add a competitive element to the challenge you may wish to divide the class into two groups or several groups and ask them to complete their section of the wall in a time limit. Then after 5 minutes they have to compare their work. They then have 1 minute to pinch ideas of the other groups. After 3 minutes the groups stop to compare their work again.

Another approach to this strategy is to draw a basic map on the sheet of paper and the students then annotate their information to the appropriate site on the map. For example there may be a local housing development taking place and the students are able to draw and annotate those areas that will be affected either positively or negatively. The same ideas could be used for a wind farm, a new road building scheme and a new out-of-town shopping area, for example.

Geography in the news displays

If you want to demonstrate just how contemporary geography is to your students and the school, you may consider having a display board that showcases the geography in the news. This display may contain news from newspaper articles, from one particular story or several. You then may have some work created by the students around the main story. To reduce your workload the onus can be placed on the students to gather the news. You may offer some type of incentive for the student who does the best job, credits, a small prize or some other type of rewards within your school system. If you have a sixth form class they should be encouraged to read the news anyway, so they should be able to provide you with current geographical stories for you to use.

Newspaper swap

Once a story is in the national newspapers, these can be used as excellent resources. If you purchase a number of newspapers these can be given to different groups of students, who then need to collect the information from the papers. There are several options open to you with this activity. You may want to group the students on ability; you could ask them to look at different aspects of the story; you may want to run the activity as a marketplace; or you may want to get the students to swap information. You could set an exam style question for the students to answer or they may use the activity as an information gathering exercise.

The benefit of buying a range of newspapers is that they can be matched to the students' abilities. Broadsheet papers can be given to high-ability students and tabloid papers can help to support lower-ability students.

News flash

Once you have taught the students some of the content surrounding a news story you are working on, the students are then shown a TV news report, but with no audio to support the images. They are then challenged to write their own news flash based on the images in the report. As the teacher you need to stop at various intervals to show the images and also to share the timings of the different sections of the report. Following is an example of a timeline from a BBC news report on the devastation caused by Hurricane Matthew.

**BBC News Report: 'Hurricane Matthew: Hundred dead in
Haiti storm disaster.'**

- 0.00–0.34: images of the destruction caused by the storm. Buildings destroyed, flooding and crops destroyed.

- 0.35–0.50: interview with a local resident

- 0.51–1.00: map of the path Hurricane Matthew took across the Atlantic Ocean

- 1.00–1.28: interview with an aid worker from the Red Cross International Aid Agency

- 1.28–2.00: images of the US Navy delivering supplies

- 2.00–2.10: images of destruction

After students are shown the report with no audio, they then have to develop their own script linked to the timeline. Students can then present their script. After the students have presented you may show them the actual report with the audio to see how closely matched their script was to the original.

Constructing case studies from geography in the news

Case studies are key elements to geographical understanding as they translate theory into real life. Aside from being a crucial part of helping students to understand the world around them, they are also fundamental to exam success. The more relevant and current the case study the better. Examiners like to see students using not only a range of case studies but also more contemporary ones. For example, if there was a volcanic eruption last week, examiners may expect to see reference made to it in the exam rather than the student trotting out the old facts and figures of the 1980 eruption of Mount Saint Helens again.

Figure 10.4 is a sheet that can be used with students to get them to record a case study from geography that is in the news. For this I get the students to use a double page in the exercise book or I provide the A3 worksheet. Students are encouraged to use colour, symbols and pictures to make their work as memorable as possible.

Using the case study recording sheet with your students

Location/background/causes

This box is used to record the accurate location of the case study. Encourage students to consider scale. Ask them to think from international to local scale: continents, countries, cities, compass direction. For example, if the case study was on the development of favelas in Brazil, students could record the following: Rocinha is located on a hillside in the south zone of Rio de Janeiro, Brazil, South America.

Background and causes may include any relevant detail that sets the scene for the case study: for example, the plates involved for an earthquake or volcano, the causes of a tropical storm, why there is a need for more housing or a new road.

Effects: primary/secondary

For this section of the sheet, students have to attempt to link ideas together. They complete the hexagons by adding one effect into each shape. They then link the hexagons by writing a connective over the lines between each shape and therefore they must be able to justify how the effects are linked together. There is space on the sheet for students to sketch in more hexagons if required. In fact, to differentiate you may choose to provide fewer or more hexagons to meet the needs of your students. For lower-attaining students you may wish to support them by completing two or three hexagons to model how to complete the sheet. To stretch and challenge your high-attaining students you may wish to add another layer of hexagons, requiring them to think deeper.

Once the hexagons are completed, provide the students with pencils or markers in three colours. The challenge is for the students to colour in the hexagons, with each colour representing a social, economic or environmental effect. If the effect could be considered both social and economic, for example, then the students can colour the hexagon half one colour and half the other. You may want to choose a colour that is created by mixing colours. For example, you may ask students to colour hexagons red for social effects, yellow for economic effects and therefore orange for socio-economic effects.

Responses and solutions

In this section of the recording sheet, students record what responses there have been to the event or scenario. Students could list the stakeholders involved in the case study for example, local residents, emergency services, local and international governments. They could then offer responses or solutions to the problem. These may be related specifically to the case study or you may ask the students to refer to other case studies to find solutions from other parts of the world. They may then be challenged to think about what might happen in the future. Are the responses and solutions sustainable?

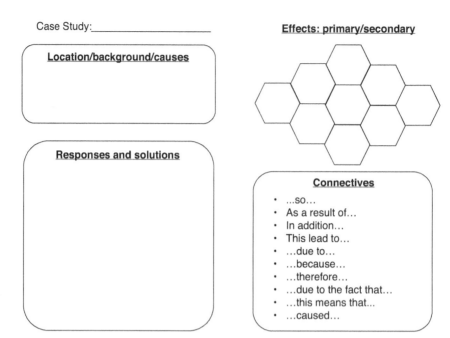

Case Study:_____

Effects: primary/secondary

Location/background/causes

Responses and solutions

Connectives

- ...so...
- As a result of...
- In addition...
- This lead to...
- ...due to...
- ...because...
- ...therefore...
- ...due to the fact that...
- ...this means that...
- ...caused...

Figure 10.4 Case study recording sheet

Geography in the news in a nutshell

- Link the students' learning to real-life situations and scenarios.
- Share news stories related to geography through displays and discussion.
- Use news events to create new case studies and examples for the students to use in assessments and exams.
- Deepen students' thinking by asking them to consider responses and solutions to new stories.

Figure 10.5 Geography in the news in a nutshell

CHAPTER 11

Teaching A Level

For many geography teachers A Level represents the epitome of teaching. It is the opportunity to develop mastery of the subject for both your students and also for yourself. A Level teaching gives you the opportunity to further develop your subject knowledge; I certainly improved my classroom practice with my GCSE classes, having taught the same topic at an A Level standard. It may also be an opportunity to trial new strategies in a 'safer' environment where you are less likely to have misbehaviour if things start to go slightly wrong. Just as A Level teaching provides a plethora of opportunities, so too does it provide a range of new challenges.

Your subject knowledge needs to be at a high-enough standard so that you can not only deliver your lessons with confidence, but also provide extension for those students who may require it. This may involve a certain amount of study if you are not familiar with the topic, since you may not have studied it since your own A Levels. Getting to grips with the rigours of the course will require time and effort in learning new assessment procedures, success criteria and course structure. It may demand a refined or even new skill set. Clearly much of this will apply not only to you as the teacher but also to your students.

You should not forget when teaching sixth-form students or further education students, that they are actually Year 11 students plus six weeks. I sometimes wonder what transformation we think will take place within the six-week holidays. What will turn that reticent, disengaged student into a model, enthusiastic, conscientious geographer? In reality, of course, little is likely to have changed. Therefore we must reassess the skill set we are expecting our A Level students to develop over the course. Hopefully, if you have mapped and developed geographical skills over the key stages, there should not be too many gaps; however an A Level course does require a new set of skills to be employed, and these skills need to be taught. I myself have fallen into the trap of making assumptions that students will somehow already know how to make notes or write essays, only to be confronted with inferior work and confused students. Therefore it is our responsibility to teach the students these skills and it is their responsibility to employ them consistently in their studies.

In addition to the skills identified in Chapter 2, the following list contains the additional key skills that A Level students require:

1 Note taking
2 Extended writing and essays
3 Using feedback to improve work
4 Reading effectively
5 Organisation

Key skill 1: note taking

The ability to make clear and concise notes is a key skill to add to the student's repertoire. The skill of picking out and distilling the key points of information is the foundation for success. When I ask students to make notes I do not expect them to copy each passage out of the textbook, word for word, though many students do. This practice requires little engagement with the text and shows little depth in the students' thinking. Before setting a note taking activity, consider what you are trying to achieve by asking the students to make notes. For me, the notes become the foundation on which all other skills, knowledge and understanding can be built so they can then apply this knowledge to exam questions. I want students to have a detailed compendium which they can refer to, to help them reignite their memory weeks, months and even years later. You may need to justify to students the relevance of taking notes, to get them to engage fully with the task, as in my experience some students may be uncooperative, questioning the benefit of making notes. As mentioned previously, notes are the foundation upon which all knowledge and understanding can be built. They act as a reminder of the main points of the topic area and the lesson. They are an important source of material for essays and also for revision. In addition, note taking promotes concentration on the topic and raises questions that can be referred to and answered in class, as well as building up an understanding of the subject.

A range of sources can be used for note taking, including:

- Textbooks
- Articles found with Internet search engines
- Newspaper articles
- Videos
- IT: podcasts, GIS, databases
- Lectures, tutorials and seminars

The following suggestions will help you to upskill your students so that they can competently and efficiently make notes in a variety of settings.

Develop study questions or challenges

Rather than having students copy out great chunks of the textbook, ask them to make notes to answer a series of questions. This requires the students to apply this knowledge and understanding to something, rather than the information gathered being classed as irrelevant or lacking purpose. It focuses their mind and their attention if the notes relate to something. Ideally use the command words from the exam board to help you craft some questions. This has three benefits: the students have study questions to make notes from; they become more au fait with the commands; they develop the knowledge and skill set to deal with and identify the meaning of those words.

For example: 'use pages 208–212 to respond to the following challenges.'

- Annotate a diagram of the structure of a tropical storm.
- Compare the primary and secondary effects of Hurricane Matthew and Typhoon Haiyan.
- Evaluate the responses of those countries affected by Hurricane Matthew.

Taking notes during the lesson

Students should get into the habit of making notes from the lesson. There may be an opportunity to do this during the lesson, or after the lesson, as part of their extra study. Note taking from lessons is a good habit to cultivate as it will stand the students in good stead for lectures at university or in further education if they decide to pursue that path. The flow chart shown in Figure 11.1 provides some guidance on how to take effective notes from lessons.

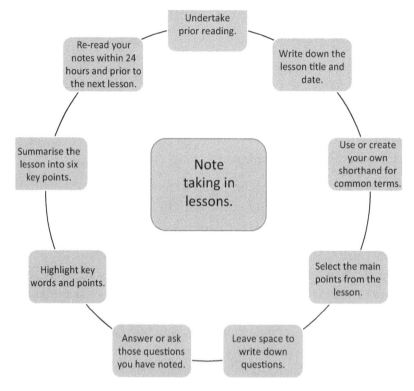

Figure 11.1 Note taking in lessons

Following are the instructions I would give to my students to help them to develop their skills. These are comprehensive instructions to help support your students to make the best, most concise and effective notes they can, in or outside of your lesson.

1 'Prior reading: to gain the most from the lesson, it is suggested that you undertake prior reading, as this will introduce you to the topic and any relevant keywords that may be used.'

2 'Write down the lesson title and date: this will help you to organise your notes and keep them chronologically. If you can turn the lesson title into a question, then you can answer it at the end. This helps you to make the lesson relevant to you and also gives the lesson a clear focus.'

3 'Use or create your own shorthand for common terms: try to abbreviate terms you use a lot, or use standard shorthand expressions for some words. Some examples are Env for environment, TS for tropical storms, Ind for industry and three dots in a triangle for "therefore".'

4　'Select the main points from the lesson: as you are listening to the teacher, note down the key points he/she is making related to the topic; these may be bullet points or in a mind map, whichever suits your style.'

5　'Leave space to write down questions: as the lesson is progressing you may find you have questions about what is being said or the text you are reading, or questions around the topic. Jot these down either in the margin or under your notes so you can refer to them later. Obviously feel free to ask any questions at any point during the lesson, but you may want to write them down to refer to the answer later.'

6　'Answer or ask those questions you have noted: if you had not had the opportunity to ask any questions during the lesson for any reason, now is the time to refer back to your notes to help you to answer those questions. You may need to reread previous lessons' notes to help you, or ask the teacher.'

7　'Highlight key points: once your notes are complete, use highlighters to pick out the keywords, ideas or concepts.'

8　'Summarise the lesson into six key points: this is a valuable part of the process because it requires you to evaluate all you have learnt during the lesson and condense that information into six key points. This act alone will help in the retention of information for the future.'

9　'Re-read your notes within 24 hours and prior to the next lesson: this is to help to cement the information into your long-term memory rather than your short-term memory, which will fade with time. Research shows that we forget 50% of what we hear within an hour, and more than 70% within two days. Even if you read only the six key points, this will help your retention of information.'

10　'Another useful activity is to compare your notes with those of your partner or another member of the class. In this way you can add any information you may have missed and clarify any points you are unsure of.'

Cornell notes

The Cornell note taking system was first developed at Cornell University in the United States. It is used by many students as a successful way to make effective and concise notes from lectures and reading materials, helping students to organise and make connections in their notes from topics, sub-topics and linked resources.

There are seven steps to making Cornell notes:

1 Prepare your note paper by dividing your page up into three sections. Draw a column down the left-hand side of your page that should take about a third of the page. This section will be used to record questions. The remaining two thirds of the page can be used to record the main points. The bottom five or six lines of the page will be used to summarise the key notes you have made, and the top six lines can be used to note down the title or learning question. See the example in Figure 11.2.

Title or Learning Question	
Questions	Key points
Summary	

Figure 11.2 An example of the Cornell notes format

2 Write down the main points of the lesson or reading material: this may be paraphrased text or summarised key points. Aim to make your sentences brief and use abbreviations or develop your own shorthand to help you. In this section should be any important dates/times/places, diagrams or pictures, tables or sketches, formulas or equations, definitions and keywords.

3 Create a series of questions related to information recorded in the notes section. Write these questions in the left-hand column.

4 Write a summary of the main ideas in your own words, or create a bullet-point list of the key concepts you have learnt.

5 Recite, cover, recall, review: recite means explaining the information in your notes out loud and in your own words; read through your notes again out loud or to someone.

6 Recall: cover the text so that all you have are the key questions in the left-hand column and, having covered the text, then answer the questions out loud.

7   Once you have answered all the questions, go back and review how well you have done. Where are there gaps in your learning? What ideas or concepts do you still need to work on?

Mind mapping

This is not a new technique, and was first developed by Tony Buzan. Done well this can be a strategy that helps students to make decisive and clear connections between topics and subject matter. Essentially mind maps are diagrams that show connections between information around a central topic or idea. At the centre of the page is the main topic area, idea or concept; branching off from this are the sub-topics or related ideas. More branches are added to the diagram to show a greater level of detail; the details can then be linked together to develop the student's ability to think synoptically.

How to create memorable mind maps

1   Starting in the centre of a blank page, draw or create an image or a picture. This picture will stimulate your imagination and help you to recall the links.

2   Connect your main branches to the central image. Use different colours for each main branch: this will help your brain to associate the colour to a particular aspect of the topic.

3   From the main branches, develop the second and third tiers of thinking and links. Use keywords or images for each branch: this helps your brain to make connections.

4   Make the whole map as colourful and creative as possible: use images throughout and keywords for each branch. The more creative the diagram, the more memorable it will be. If you can make your mind map as interesting as possible, it is far more likely that it will aid recall and cement the information to your long-term memory.

5   Rather than simply file your mind map away, display it in a prominent place, next to a light switch, on the fridge door or above your desk. Then, after a few weeks, you could take it down and test your recall by trying to draw the mind map again from memory.

Key skill 2: extended writing and essays

For A Level students, writing extended answers and essays probably causes the most anxiety and discomfort. The main reason for this is because it is often a skill not previously encountered. The thought of having to write three or four A4 pages, without any resources to help them, can be a scary notion because it is outside of their comfort zone. However all we have to do is extend their zone of comfort through regular practice, rehearsal and support, and their confidence will grow. Thus what was once considered to be daunting now becomes habitual.

For students to become successful at A Level then, they need to have developed a deep understanding of the subject matter; to be able to recognise linkages between topics, concepts and ideas and then be able to communicate this understanding in their writing. Not only must they develop their concise and coherent written communication skills, but they also need to apply their knowledge and understanding with an increased capacity to argue, evaluate and write with synopticity. It is this ability to articulate their knowledge and understanding that many students find so difficult – but it is a skill, and as with any skill it can be taught and developed over time.

As with any new skill, the aim is to give the student clear and structured support to begin with; as the student develops his/her skill in this area, this support and scaffold can be withdrawn. The student will then have the independence and skill set to be confident when responding to more challenging questions.

What does the question mean?

A starting point is unpicking the question. Students need to develop the skill of interpreting the question so that they know exactly what they are being asked to do or write about. This starts with the command word. Command words are the words and phrases used in exams, and other assessment tasks, that tell students how they should answer the question. The exam board will provide a list of command words with definitions for you to use. Following are some examples of command words used by the Assessment and Qualifications Alliance (AQA) examination board:

Analyse: break down concepts, information and/or issues to convey an understanding of them by finding connections and causes and/or effects.

Annotate: add to a diagram, image or graphic a number of words that describe and/or explain features, rather than just identify them (which is labelling).

Assess: consider several options or arguments and weigh them up so as to come to a conclusion about their effectiveness or validity.

Compare: describe the similarities and differences of at least two phenomena.

Comment on: make a statement that arises from a factual point made – add a view, an opinion or an interpretation. In data/stimulus response questions, examine the stimulus material provided and then make statements about the material and its content that are relevant, appropriate and geographical, but not directly evident.

Contrast: point out the differences between at least two phenomena.

Define . . . what is meant by . . .: state the precise meaning of an idea or concept.

Describe: give an account in words of a phenomenon which may be an entity, an event, a feature, a pattern, a distribution or a process. For example, if describing a landform, say what it looks like and give some indication of size or scale, what it is made of and where it is in relation to something else (field relationship).

Discuss: set out both sides of an argument (for and against), and come to a conclusion related to the content and emphasis of the discussion. There should be some evidence of balance, though not necessarily of equal weighting.

Evaluate: consider several options, ideas or arguments and form a view based on evidence about their importance/validity/merit/utility.

Examine: consider carefully and provide a detailed account of the indicated topic.

Explain . . . , Why? Suggest reasons for . . .: set out the causes of a phenomenon and/or the factors which influence its form/nature. This usually requires an understanding of processes.

Justify: give reasons for the validity of a view or idea or why some action should be undertaken. This might reasonably involve discussing and discounting alternative views or actions.

To what extent: form and express a view as to the merit or validity of a view or statement after examining the evidence available and/or different sides of an argument.

The command words offer a range of challenges for the students. It is the interpretation of these words which will ultimately dictate the success of the answer the students then proceed to write. Thus, understanding these terms is paramount to the achievement of the students. When introducing them to the students, I begin by asking them to group the terms into three levels of difficulty: low, middle and high-order thinking. Which terms do they think are the hardest to interpret and which terms are they confident with? I produced Table 11.1 to help students to recognise the increasing level of challenge presented by the terms.

Table 11.1 Command words and levels of thinking

Low-order thinking	Middle-order thinking	High-order thinking
This involves recall of facts, terms, basic concepts and answers.	Application of acquired knowledge, examining and dissecting information into parts, for example causes, effects and responses. Making some inference and finding evidence to support the answer.	Linking of concepts and ideas. Presents and defends opinions by making judgements about information. Questions the validity of information and evaluates ideas. Synopticity is used to develop high-order geographical thinking.
• Define . . . what is meant by . . . • Describe	• Annotate • Compare • Comment on • Contrast • Distinguish between • Explain . . . , Why . . . ? Suggest reasons for . . . • Outline . . . , summarise . . .	• Critically assess • Discuss • Evaluate • Examine • Interpret • Justify • To what extent

Once students have recognised the increasing level of challenge presented by the command words, they aim to get a deeper understanding of what they mean, and therefore have a better grasp of what they are being asked to do in the question.

Modelling

When I first ask my students to write extended answers or essays I begin by modelling good practice. I start by dissecting the exam question into the relevant parts. These are the command word/s, the topic, the focus of the question and any key terms I feel need defining. After I have written the question on the board, we start to annotate the question with a green pen. I ask the students to identify the command word and ask them to explain what it means. I ask them to put this into language that it is easier to understand at this stage. Figure 11.3

is an example of an exam question where the student has identified the command words and explained what the command word means. In addition they have then highlighted the other key aspects to the question.

'Technology is the best way to reduce the impact of an earthquake'. To what extent do you agree with this view? (AQA 2015).

> This means: I have to give my own view based on evidence.
>
> I have to say how valid an idea is. In this case, how valid is it that technology can reduce the impacts of earthquakes?
>
> I need to consider both sides of the argument.

Figure 11.3 Recognising command words

The next stage is to highlight and annotate the key terms, topic and focus of the question. You can demonstrate this by asking the students to give you synonyms for the key terms. In this example I would ask the students the following:

'What do we mean by technology?' Equipment, designs, skills, techniques, processes.

'Give me another word for impact.' Effects, consequences, the results of . . .

'Define an earthquake.' A release of pressure.

The student responses are then recorded on the board and the students annotate their own copy of the question. Figure 11.4 is an example of how a dissected question may look.

Having dissected the question down into the three main parts: command word, topic and focus of the question, the students are then given the opportunity to plan their essay. As previously mentioned, for their first essay I will guide them through the process with no time constraints and then, as they develop their skills, I will expect them to plan the essay in approximately 5 minutes.

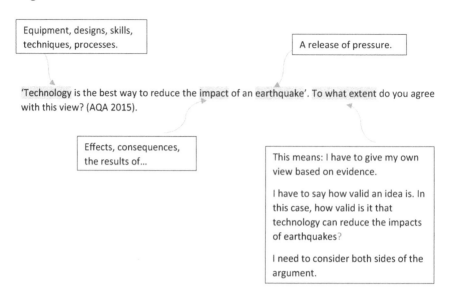

Equipment, designs, skills, techniques, processes.

A release of pressure.

'Technology is the best way to reduce the impact of an earthquake'. To what extent do you agree with this view? (AQA 2015).

Effects, consequences, the results of...

This means: I have to give my own view based on evidence.

I have to say how valid an idea is. In this case, how valid is it that technology can reduce the impacts of earthquakes?

I need to consider both sides of the argument.

Figure 11.4 Dissecting the question

Begin by asking the students to define any of the keywords in the question: the aim is to make these as comprehensive and detailed as possible. The plan will then involve the students considering which sections of any relevant case studies they will be using. Students will often learn a plethora of case studies, and it is important for them to recognise that often just knowing a few in great depth allows them to apply different parts of the case study to pretty much any question on that topic. For example, learning an in-depth case study on the eruptions of Mount Etna would support the student in answering any of the following exam-type questions based on the following topics:

- Features of plate margins
- Landforms associated with plate movement
- Volcanic hazards
- Frequency of volcanic hazards
- Impacts of volcanic hazards
- Management of volcanic hazards

Students could apply their knowledge of Mount Etna to help them answer questions on any of the topic areas listed: it gives them the evidence to support their points and helps them to write with authority about the topic.

Following is a structure that you may use with your students to help them craft their essay responses.

Introduction

This is where the student needs to define any keywords or terminology from within the question. This does not have to be a lengthy section; in fact it should be restricted to one paragraph, with any main points outlined concisely.

Middle

It is important to stress to the students that each paragraph should contain one key idea related to the question, and the first sentence should contain the main point of the paragraph. This main point should then be backed up with an example or evidence. This is when students can apply their knowledge and understanding gleaned from their case study material. To help students to think like a geographer they can employ the acronym SPEEDS (social, political, economic, environmental, demographic, scale). This requires the students to think how each area is connected to the topic or focus of the question. How does the issue affect the people or society? What political decision will need to be made as a result of the issues? How does it affect the economy, job creation and government spending? How will it affect the environment, for better or worse? What demographic or groups of people will be affected? Will they be affected in different ways? How will it affect the elderly, the unemployed, the under 16s? How will it affect areas at different scales globally, internationally, nationally and locally? If students have been considering these questions, then they should be in a good position to link their ideas together, and to add the elements of synopticity. As was earlier defined, synopticity is 'an understanding of how human and physical geographies interact'. Yet this definition can be developed to include the understanding that it is also the students' ability to draw on their understanding of the connections between human and physical geographies. In essence it is their ability to 'think like a geographer'. Students need to make links between physical, human and environmental geography, and to identify patterns and processes at a variety of scales. This ability to think synoptically is what identifies the most able geographers, yet this is a skill that can be developed rather than an intrinsic skill possessed by the few.

Conclusion

The better conclusions show that the students are considering future developments and potential scenarios; for example, they consider what influences climate change may play in the future or future political changes in decision making and policy. They consider sustainability and how situations or issues can be managed in a sustainable way, thus providing for future generations. This future perspective can often offer a new slant for the essay rather than regurgitating the same facts from previous paragraphs. It also serves as a tidy ending and conclusion to many essays. The conclusion is also an opportunity to allow the students to convey their own thoughts on the question and reach a valid decision.

When developing the students' writing habits, it is also important to emphasise the conventions of geographical writing, and some of the more technical aspects of essay construction. When working with my class on extended writing I share the following key points to note with the students:

- In a geographical essay, it is important to remember not to include value judgements. These are statements based upon your own beliefs and are not necessarily quantified by any evidence. Never use 'I' or make personal statements – e.g. 'I think globalisation is terrible' or 'Deforestation is a bad thing.'

- Refer to any diagrams you may have drawn in your essay. 'As you can see in the diagram above/below . . .'

- Vary the length of your sentences. Start paragraphs with short sentences and develop your writing from that starting point.

- Keep your paragraphs short and keep to one topic or idea in each paragraph. This makes it easy for the examiner to read.

- Skip a line between paragraphs. This makes it far easier to read and follow the sequence of the essay and therefore it is easier for the examiner to mark it.

Extended writing and essay planning

If the students want to be successful then they need to plan for success. Planning extended writing and essays involves more than they may realise when they start. They need to consider a range of ideas and then synthesise these into one clear and coherent plan. The essay plan shown in Figure 11.5 aims to help the students to think about each aspect of the essay, from dissecting the question to how to develop their synopticity. Having used this with many students in the past I know how it has helped them to clarify their thinking and develop a clear plan for their essay.

Title:

Command word:	Key words and topic:	Focus:

Beginning:

Definition of key terms:_____
_____
_____
_____

Which case studies/evidence you will use:_____
_____
_____
_____
_____

Middle:

Each paragraph should have one key idea.

The first sentence of each paragraph should state the main point.

Support your idea with examples or evidence.

Develop arguments logically.

Refer back to the question .

Synopticity! Link ideas together.

S.P.E.E.D

Social

Political

Economic

Environmental

Demographic

Conclusion:

Figure 11.5 Essay plan

As students become more au fait with the planning process they may need to make few notes under the relevant sections. The aim is for the students to become unconsciously competent when defining command words – i.e. that it should become almost automatic for them to be able to decipher command words, pick out the topic and understand the focus of the question without having to ponder over each term for any great length of time. Thus the support required becomes less and less as they develop the habit of planning essays. Obviously some students will take a longer time to grasp the main crux of the exercise, and these students could be provided with extra support such as sentence stems or paragraph starters to help them embed the skills.

Marking and feedback to extended responses and essays

When marking students' work it is worthwhile using either the exam board's abbreviations or your own code to help students to recognise where their work has met specific criteria or where their work needs developing or improving. Marking abbreviations may be different for different exam boards. Table 11.2 provides a code that I use with my students which draws on a number of good practice techniques.

Table 11.2 Marking abbreviations

Abbreviation	Meaning
AO1	Where the students demonstrate their knowledge and understanding of geographical concepts or ideas, places and environments, interactions and changes, at a variety of scales.
AO2	Where the students apply their knowledge and understanding in different contexts. They show they can evaluate, analyse and interpret geographical information and issues.
Rep	Repetition of the same point
V	Vague
VJ	Value judgement (including your own personal values to an issue)
Sp	Spelling mistake
P	Punctuation mistake
G	Grammar mistake
//	New paragraph
DP+	Developed the point well
DP–	Need to develop the point more

Employing the abbreviations should help to reduce your marking time yet still enable you to make your points clearly.

Key skill 3: using feedback to improve work

Having marked the students' essays, you now need to take time to go through the work with them. This feedback is an opportunity to reflect on what went well and what students can do to improve their work. I use a visualiser to project parts of students' essays onto the boards so that together we can unpick what made that section of the essay so good or what could be added to improve it. This is a valuable exercise, as students learn from good practice, noticing what the better answers include and also how they are structured.

Another approach is to give students an essay to read through that earned one grade above their own. For example, ask a student who scored a D grade in their essay to look and read through an essay that scored a C. This helps students to recognise that their own essay probably only required a few tweaks or additions to reach the next grade. This is preferable to giving the student an A grade piece of work which may well leave him/her thinking that an A is unachievable. Then, as the students continue to progress, they may come to realise that by learning the necessary skills and developing the required knowledge and understanding they too can achieve at the very highest level. Figure 11.10 is a template that I use with A Level students to help them to reflect on their current practice when writing extended answers and essays.

Essay autopsy

I start by projecting the mark scheme onto the board as well as providing a copy for the students to look at. I then talk through both a student response to the essay title and how the marks were allocated for the question from the mark scheme. Students annotate their work with content or pieces of information that they could have included into their essays to improve their work. This may include ideas or concepts, or facts and figures from a case study. Then, having completed this, I ask the students to re-read their answer and use three different coloured highlighters to highlight the use of keywords, where they have linked their ideas together and where they have referred back to the question. This provides the students with a visual picture and pattern of when they have met the three criteria. It acts as a very clear indication of which areas they are deficient in and what they need to do to improve. For example, when I first carry out this exercise in many cases it is clear that students refer to the exam question only at the start and at the end of the essay. The essay often shows the lack of linked ideas. As you employ this exercise after every extended answer, the students soon realise that it is imperative to meet the three criteria and thus the habit develops to include key terms, link ideas and refer back to the question consistently.

Ten outstanding ways to develop students' extended writing

Essay go' round

For this activity the students are divided into groups; each group is given a different essay title or an extended question on flip chart paper or a large sheet of paper. The first group then has approximately 5 minutes to deconstruct and annotate the question including command words, the topic area, the focus question and to define any keywords. After the 5 minutes have elapsed the question is passed on to the next group. They then have 5 minutes to plan the response on the paper, then again after 5 minutes the question is passed on to the next group to craft the first paragraph. Then depending upon the number of groups you have you may want to select an activity from the following list:

- The next group writes another paragraph.
- The next group can use their notes and textbooks to add to the answer.
- The next group writes a conclusion.
- The next group writes and answers the question in 100 words.
- The next group writes an answer to the question in 50 words.
- The next group writes the mark scheme for the question.

There is a variety of ways in which this activity can be used, and there is no hard and fast rule on how it should be done; tailor it to meet your students' needs. They may need more time to research the answer; or they may want to spend time on it to create a model answer that can then be distributed to the whole class.

Mix and match

I suggest you keep a copy of a range of essays from previous years that you can use with your class. Use an essay either from the Internet, from a previous class or one you have written, and cut it up into different sections. The students' challenge is then to work out how it is structured and how it fits back together. You will need to cut and paste the document on the computer otherwise it will simply become a jigsaw for the students, which lacks the rigour you are seeking. Having completed the challenge, ask the students to recognise the pattern of the essay. If the essay is a model example, then it should follow a similar pattern to the essay plan (see Figure 11.5), state the main point, use evidence as support and refer back to the question. You could ask them to redraft part of the essay with improvements. Students could highlight in three different colours where there is evidence of keywords and linked ideas, and where the answer refers back to the question.

Word cloud

Word clouds are fantastic for engaging students and also for challenging them to think more deeply. Students are presented with a word cloud that contains exam command words and key topic words. The challenge is then to construct an exam-style question and an answer including some of the key topic words from the cloud. In my experience students really enjoy this activity and relish the challenge of constructing both the question and the answer. Figure 11.6 is an example of a word cloud created for the topic of tectonic hazards.

Student examiner

Students are given a number of essays or extended responses from students from previous years. The challenge is for the students to then judge which essay they consider to be the best and why. Using the mark scheme, they can begin to recognise which qualities are included in the better responses. The purpose of this active analysis is for students to reflect on not just the examples but also their own essays, understanding the criteria that need to be met to move up to the next grade boundary. Students may be tasked with ranking or grading the essays. Ask them to justify their rank: why is Answer 1 better than Answer 2?

Hexagonal thinking

This activity is superb in developing the student's ability to link ideas and concepts together. Students are given approximately ten hexagon shapes that they can write in. Then the class is presented with either an extended question or a topic theme. The students' challenge is to write their key points onto their hexagons, and then as a class the students must arrange the hexagons to make links between the different key points. This can be done individually, in

Figure 11.6 Tectonic hazards word cloud

pairs or as a whole class exercise. The main benefit of this strategy is that the students get to visually see how ideas can be linked together and how connections can be made between concepts and ideas.

Speed writing

The purpose of this activity is to engage the students with writing fluently, generating ideas and writing under time constraints. The premise is that the students are allotted a short amount of time to either answer a question or write all they know on a particular subject. Students are given the following instructions:

1   Write as fast as you can until the teacher says 'stop'.
2   Don't lift your pen off the paper.
3   No corrections are allowed.
4   When you have been told to stop, then count the number of words you have written in the allotted time.

Explain to the students that the purpose of the exercise is for them to write down all they know on a particular topic or subject. They should not worry about spelling, repetition or grammar at this stage. Once the students have stopped writing, ask them to count up the total number of words; this will give you an indication of how well the students are able to write under pressure and also how well they can recall their knowledge on the subject matter. You can then discuss what the students have written and how their work is structured. You may wish to draw their attention to how well they have organised their ideas. I often ask my students to then highlight linked ideas so that they can recognise where they have been able to develop their point. You may wish to use this work as a starting point for the students to then go on to write a more polished piece of written work. Alternatively you could ask the students to work together to write one collaborative paragraph on the topic.

This activity can be used in a variety of settings. For example:

- Prewriting before an essay to formulate ideas.
- Reviewing what the students remember about a topic.
- Reviewing what the students can remember about the lesson.

As an extension you may want to challenge the students to see how much more they can add to their work within another minute. You can create a competition: 'Who can write the most about eco-systems in 1 minute?'

Ideas generator

Students are provided with the ideas generator sheet (see Figure 11.7). This aims to stimulate the students into thinking more deeply about their essay content, and also generate ideas for what they could include in their work to make it even better. The questions on the sheet are generic questions that can

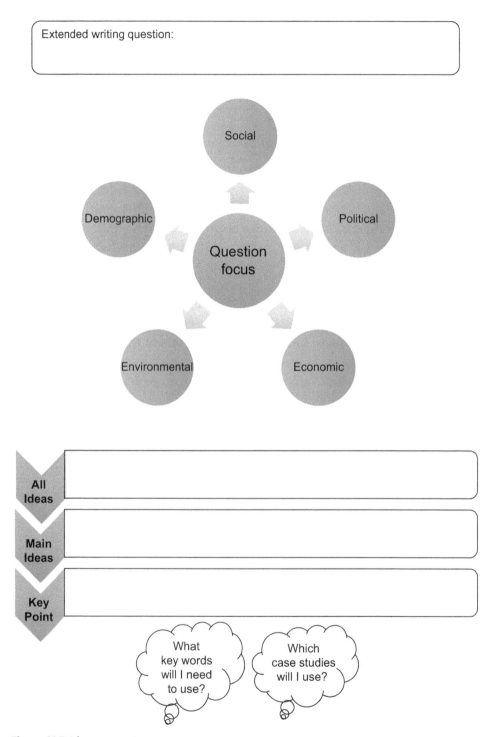

Figure 11.7 Ideas generator

be applied to any topic; however, you may ask the students to also consider topic-specific questions they could ask.

This technique can be applied at a number of stages of the writing process. You may use it during the planning process, in conjunction with 'speed writing' or as a feedback tool after they have completed their essay to get the students to consider what else they could have included to improve their work. Students can work in pairs or groups: they pass their work to another student who then writes appropriate questions about the text in the margins. Once the work is returned you may want the students to then either answer those questions or at least consider them before moving on. The ultimate aim is for the support sheet to be withdrawn as the students develop the habits of asking their own internal questions.

Storyboards

The storyboard strategy is nothing new in the classroom; however, rather than using this technique to purely tell a story it can be applied to an exam question to demonstrate links between concepts both visually and in writing. The basic premise is that students draw a sequence of boxes, and they then have to either draw or find a picture that can be used to represent the idea or concept. This then must link to the next box in the sequence. This technique offers a variety of opportunities: you could provide the students with the pictures that they have to then link into a sequence, you could set them a homework to collect pictures to be used in the following lesson or you may want to ask your students to draw their own pictures or diagrams. The students could use their file paper, their books, the desk or even the back of some old wallpaper stuck to the wall to get them to show the links they have developed. It is the creation process that helps to ingrain ideas to develop a deeper understanding.

This very visual approach to idea development and synopticity can be beneficial to your students. Giving them a visual representation of the idea, process or concept can help students to improve their memory and also recognise the links between difficult theoretical concepts.

Literacy mats

Offering literacy, word or topic mats can be a much-needed support for students, especially those low-attaining students who require support and structure to encourage them to write with extension and to link ideas together. Figure 11.8

How to write with synopticity

Case studies/examples

Aim to qualify your main points with examples or case study materials. This doesn't mean you have to write everything you know on a particular study, rather that you need to select the relevant information from your case study to support your point.

Make your examples as relevant and as current as possible.

Application

Apply your knowledge and understanding of key concepts to the question. Demonstrate your knowledge and understanding of places, processes and environments by including detail throughout, making your points relevant and appropriate to the question.

Make links

Linking ideas together is crucial to helping you develop your point. Make links between topics, processes, places, issues, human, physical and environmental and economic geographies. How does the issue, scenario or challenge effect on a social, political, economic, environmental and demographic level?

Compare

Consider comparing regions or countries. What comparisons can you make for areas facing the same issue or challenges? Do they deal with the same challenge in different ways?

Contrast

Recognise the contrast that exists between countries at different levels of economic development. For example: HICs LICs NEE, BRICs. Also consider the contrast within a country for example rural and urban areas within the same country.

Scale

Think in terms of both time and geographical scale.

Timescale: think frequency, periodicity, changes over time.

Geographical scale: think global, international, national, regional, local.

Future

In the conclusion consider what might happen in the future. How will things change? Are there issues around sustainability? Climate change? Developments in technology?

Figure 11.8 How to write with synopticity

is an example that supports students in understanding the elements of synopticity. I also use a generic literacy mat that has a number of useful connectives that can help students to link ideas.

Using feedback to improve students' work

I often remind the students that it is not the lessons where they write their essays that are the most important but the feedback lesson afterwards. This is the opportunity to reflect on what the students did well and also what the students need to do to improve their skills, knowledge and understanding. Having emphasised the importance to the students I give them time to reflect on their work; if they have been given essays or tests back I allow them time to look through their work and discuss grades with each other, as they always like to find out how their peers have got on.

Feedback must always be related to some sort of success criteria. Otherwise, how are the students to know what they need to do to get to the next level or grade? The success criteria will often take the form of the exam mark scheme. Figure 11.9 is an example of a mark scheme matrix that I have adapted to demonstrate to the students the content and skills they need to display, in order to work through the different levels. It is used for twenty-mark questions and, although it may not directly apply to every twenty-mark question, there are twenty boxes that may help you to show the students exactly why they achieved the mark they did. The left-hand column can be used to offer some direction on what the students need to do to improve their work.

Self-assessment

This is a key part of student progress: getting the students to recognise their own mistakes and to understand which areas they need to develop. Asking students to assess their own performance challenges them to consider not only their own motivation and effort towards the task, but also their awareness of the success criteria they are being tested against. Hopefully, as the students have progressed throughout their time at school, they have developed their own self-awareness and honesty about their work. Being able to take responsibility for their results is a key attribute that successful students possess. Rather than blaming the teacher, the time limit or the lack of resources, students who can take full responsibility are those more likely to gain the most from the feedback process, accepting where they made mistakes and then having the desire and tenacity to want to put them right next time. The self-assessment

A level geography extended answer feedback sheet

	Concepts and processes	Case studies	Analysis and evaluation	Scale	Conclusion
Improve it Key terms Case studies	Very limited and rarely logical evidence of links between knowledge and understanding to the application of knowledge and understanding in different contexts.	Very limited relevant knowledge and understanding of place and environments.	Very limited analysis and evaluation in the application of knowledge and understanding. This lacks clarity and coherence.	Very limited awareness of scale and temporal change. There are several inaccuracies.	Very limited and/or unsupported evaluative conclusion that is loosely based on knowledge and understanding which is applied to the context of the question.
Address the question Repetition Structure	Some evidence of links between knowledge and understanding to the application of knowledge and understanding in different contexts.	Some relevant knowledge and understanding of place and environments.	Some partially relevant analysis and evaluation in the application of knowledge and understanding.	Some awareness of scale and temporal change which is integrated where appropriate. There may be a few inaccuracies.	Some sense of an evaluative conclusion partially based upon knowledge and understanding which is applied to the context of the question.
Command words Vague	Generally clear evidence of links between knowledge and understanding to the application of knowledge and understanding in different contexts.	Generally clear and relevant knowledge and understanding of place and environments.	Generally clear, coherent and relevant analysis and evaluation in the application of knowledge and understanding.	Generally clear awareness of scale and temporal change which is integrated where appropriate.	Clear and evaluative conclusion that is based on knowledge and understanding which is applied to the context of the question.
Understanding of key concepts Literacy	Full evidence of links between knowledge and understanding to the application of knowledge and understanding in different contexts.	Detailed and highly relevant and appropriate knowledge and understanding of place and environments used throughout.	Detailed coherent and relevant analysis and evaluation in the application of knowledge and understanding throughout.	Detailed awareness of scale and temporal change which is well integrated where appropriate.	Detailed evaluative conclusion which is rational and based firmly on knowledge and understanding. This is applied to the context of the question.

Figure 11.9 Mark scheme matrix

sheet in Figure 11.10 contains a number of developmental questions that can help your students progress after every assessed piece of work.

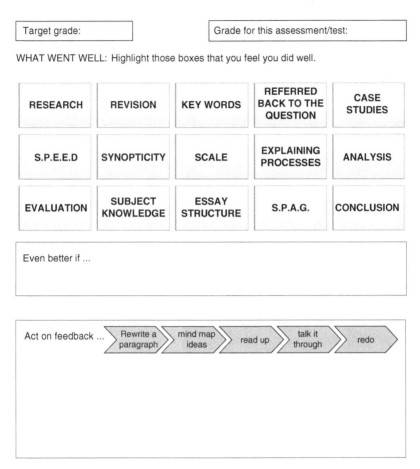

Figure 11.10 A Level self-assessment sheet

Key skill 4: reading effectively

One of the key skills that students in further education may be deficient in is the understanding of the need for wider reading. If geography students do not undertake purposeful and effective reading, it is likely that they will not have developed the adequate depth of knowledge and understanding to enable them to achieve at the highest level. Thus an emphasis on reading effectively is vital if you are to support your students to perform at their best.

The majority of text that your students will encounter will be non-fiction, and effectively reading this text may require a different set of skills than those needed to analyse fiction. Also the depth at which you require your students to read will vary from text to text. Do you want them to simply scan the text for an answer, or do you need them to investigate and analyse text to draw conclusions and/or learn a new concept?

Reading effectively presents a number of challenges for the teacher. First, it is difficult to gauge a student's prior knowledge and understanding of text. Often geographical text builds and relies on background knowledge. This is fine if the students have that broad depth of knowledge already in place; yet for some students presented with new text it may simply serve to confuse and overwhelm them. So the challenge for us as teachers is to find ways to help students unlock the text and improve their absorption rate (the rate at which students are able to assimilate new knowledge as they read).

Strategies to improve a student's absorption rate and understanding

Multiple texts

One way to improve students' understanding of a topic is to ask them to read a number of texts on a topic so that their reading will result in a higher level of knowledge absorption. This will help to embed the knowledge you seek to gain for the student. Reading should focus around a *primary text*. The primary text may be the principal reading material for the class, often the course textbook, onto which you bolt the supplementary text or articles to support the learning around that topic. Supplementary texts may provide background that is easier to access, show a contrasting viewpoint or develop a new strand of thinking around the topic. For example, you may use an A Level textbook to provide some context and background knowledge for your students to then build on with the supplementary texts such as journals and articles. When considering the topic of climate change, for instance, you may provide a range of texts from contrasting viewpoints, proving or disproving the issue, and asking the students to identify bias in the text and why that may be so.

Reading goal

Establish a purpose for the students. Ask them to read to answer a particular question or to develop knowledge and understanding to add to an essay or extended question. Having a reading goal helps to prioritise the information and this focus can aid the absorption rate.

Distilled reading

This technique requires the student to read a passage of text and then extract the most essential aspects of the text. This may be summarised in a paragraph or you may ask the students to write down what they have learnt from the text in fifty words. This requires higher-level thinking as they must now prioritise their thinking into the most salient points.

Reading with a pen

Encourage the students to read with a pen and highlighter. They can highlight key points, terms and text as they see fit. Then ask students to jot down questions they may have whilst reading, or ask them to make links between what they are reading to other aspects of the topic or the course. Students may want to write their own explanations to concepts in the book's margins or at the bottom or top of pages. Putting difficult concepts into their own words will help them when they refer to the text later.

SQ3R

This reading method, first developed back in 1946, still has relevance to today's classroom. It has been attributed to Francis Robinson, and requires students to Skim or Survey the text, Question, and then Read, Recite and Review (hence SQ3R). The aim of this technique is to help students to remember key text in a systematic way.

Skim or Survey: Ask students to glance over the text to gain an overview of the topic/concepts being covered. This will help them to grasp the main ideas before they begin to read the text in depth. The students can highlight keywords or text they feel sum up the main thrust of the chapter or section.

Question: Students are required to formulate questions about the text. They can turn headings and sub headings into questions. You can support students by giving them the following question stems: who, what, when, where, why and how.

Read: The students now read the text with the questions in mind. As they read they should be attempting to answer the question/questions they have raised. Try to summarise the key points as you read.

Recite: This is the opportunity for students to answer the questions raised. Notes can be made to answer the questions and keywords highlighted. Students should be given the opportunity to recite what they have learnt.

Review: This is a key and much overlooked section of the process. It is vital that the notes, questions and answers you have made are reviewed in order to enhance knowledge retention. This may be rereading the notes within the next twenty four hours, or may involve creating flash cards on the topic. Whatever method the students use it is imperative that they review their work. What were the key points? If you had to summarise the text in twenty words what would they be? Summarise the passage in one word. This can be discussed in pairs, as a class, written down or simply orally.

Topic: _____

Chapter/Section:
Skim/Survey: Skim through the text and note down: titles, subtitles, key words that stick in your head at the first glance.

Questions: Turn the headings and subheadings into questions. Who, What, When, Where, Why, How, How ought.	**Recite:** Answer the questions you have developed from the text.

READ

Review: Summarise the text in 20 words or less. What are the key points?

Figure 11.11 SQ3R reading template

Key skill 5: organisation

As previously mentioned, I think as teachers we often make the assumption that when students become sixth formers they automatically change into highly motivated, conscientious and effective students. In reality they are Year 11 students plus six weeks and thus will require the support we can offer to mould them into the academic students we need them to be in order to be successful in our subject. A key attribute to develop is that of organisation.

As A Level students often have more 'free time' and independence within the school framework, it is necessary for them to understand how they can organise and manage their time most efficiently. Following are a number of strategies and techniques to help your students.

Notes

It is often the case that at A Level you require the students to use a folder to keep all their work and notes in. This can present a unique challenge for some students. If they have never used folders before and relied on exercise books, then the idea of having to transfer work and organise notes and sheets chronologically can be alien to them. As the teacher it is important to share your expectations with the students. How do you want their folders or notes to look? Do you want dividers between topics? Separate folders for physical and human geography? Different folders for different teachers, perhaps? It is good practice to have folder checklists for your students to use, or details of what should be in their folders. This may include the following:

• Specification content
• Notes on theory
• Glossary of key terms
• Homework assignments (flipped learning, booklets)
• Assessments (exam practice questions, past papers)
• Assessment feedback sheets
• Self-assessment sheets
• Tracking sheets
• Further reading

Depending upon your cohort, you may want to give the students the opportunity to use an exercise book. I have found this most effective with low-attaining students who struggle with organisation. Having notes that follow on lesson after lesson has helped them to remain organised, rather than having to transfer notes and sheets to folders which may get misplaced or lost. Whether your students use folders or books, I suggest regular checks.

Getting work completed

One of the biggest barriers faced by sixth-form students is the increased demand to get work completed independently, and also meeting tight deadlines with a more substantial work load. To meet all the demands and rigours of A Level it is important to employ an effective time management system that works. A tried and tested method used by many successful people is to create an action plan, in other words a 'to do' list.

'To do' lists can take on several forms and guises, but essentially it is a good idea to start with the bigger picture and then break this down into daily goals: for example you can help your students by supporting them to make long term, monthly and daily plans. These may include the following.

Long-term plan

- Dates of final exams
- Dates of mock exams
- Dates of fieldwork
- Deadlines for fieldwork investigations
- Half term and termly holidays
- Important dates from the school calendar

Medium (monthly) plan

- What will be covered in the specification
- Deadlines for essays/assignments/homework and notes
- Exam practice questions/papers

Daily plan

- Which work needs to be done (broken down into smaller sections)
- Study sessions
- 'Free lessons': which work will be done during this time?

As a teacher you are able to provide some support and guidance with the long-term or monthly plan; however the students must take responsibility for their daily action plan or 'to do' list. Once they have made their list of all the things that they need to accomplish, both academic and personal, they then need to prioritise their tasks. They can do this by asking the following questions:

- What is my most important task?
- If I could only complete just one thing on this list, what would it be?
- What is the most valuable use of my time?

This helps to crystallise the most important task. Then the student categorises this as 'number one' working his/her way down the list, numbering tasks as he/she sees fit. Once the tasks are ranked, the students must get to work on the first task. They may need to break their number-one task down further by writing down all the steps necessary to complete the top challenge, and then again prioritise these sub-tasks. These will help to formulate their daily duties and give clarity to what they need to accomplish. Prioritising tasks can be a challenge in itself, so teaching the students how to do this can be a useful skill for them to develop. I use the 'President Eisenhower' method. This is useful when you are faced with a number of different demands, all of which appear essential at the time, yet with some thought you may be able to prioritise the tasks.

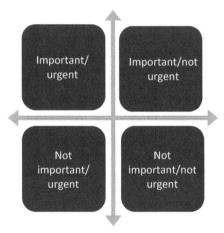

Figure 11.12 Prioritising matrix

As can be seen from the matrix shown in Figure 11.12 all tasks are ranked depending upon their importance and urgency. All tasks can be assigned to a box on the matrix. Let's look at a typical student's example:

- An essay the student forgot about and needs to be handed in tomorrow: important and urgent

- The student's university application for next year: important but not urgent

- The student needs to return a reply slip of some nature: urgent but not important

- All other tasks that fall into the not urgent and not important are those tasks you tackle last, if at all. The students must ask themselves: if the chore is not urgent and not important does it need to be done?

Having worked out which tasks are most important and most urgent, the students work on their top priority, working their way down the list. A key habit to develop, whilst working on tasks, is concentration. Once they start a task they need to stick with it until it is completed. Once your students have completed a task, however, encourage them to rewards themselves, either with an episode of their favourite TV show or time spent on their phone.

Deadlines

Give students realistic and achievable deadlines. Make sure they make a note of when the deadline is, either in their smartphones, planners or other devices they may use. Discuss what is expected and even show them model work so that they are all clear about your expectations.

Distraction-free environments

Speak to the students about the need to establish distraction-free environments. If students are to give themselves a fighting chance of accomplishing their goals then they need to be willing to give time and concentration to the task. This cannot be achieved if they are trying to write an essay in the sixth form common room, or answer difficult questions whilst continually looking at the phone. The idea that this generation of students can multitask is a myth. The brain isn't wired to be able to do multiple tasks to a high standard. Yes, it is possible to do several things at once, but it is not possible to do several things at once well. Therefore encourage students to switch off their mobile phones, TVs or other electronic devices that may distract them from their priority task. The added benefit is that if the students are concentrating on just one task at a time this will, more often than not, speed up the whole process.

Synergy

This is the interaction of elements that, when combined, produce a total effect that is greater than the sum of all the individual elements. It is often described as being 2 + 2 = 5. Encourage students to set up study groups: the sharing of ideas and resources can be a very powerful tool to bring about real improvement in students' attainment. My A Level students have not only taken it upon themselves to set up a dedicated time in the week to discuss their homework together, but they have also set up 'group chats' using their mobile phones so they can share ideas or articles, or post resources. The benefit of this cannot be measured. Having students teach each other or work together to solve problems is a valuable exercise from which they all gain, and of course helps them to develop their geographical skills, knowledge and understanding.

Figure 11.13 summarises the key points of this chapter.

A Level teaching in a nutshell

- Remember that the students are Year 11s plus six weeks.
- Don't assume they will have the necessary skills to be successful. You will have to teach them if you haven't done so already.
- Spend time developing the key skills of note taking, extended writing, using feedback, effective reading and organisational skills.
- Develop a dialogue with the students so you can identify issues early.
- Check their folders regularly to ensure their notes are to the standard you require.

Figure 11.13 A Level teaching in a nutshell

CHAPTER 12

Marking for progress

There is little that creates more controversy and angst in teaching than discussions around marking and assessment. I think this is because so many of us – if not all of us – as teachers have such strong views on the subject. I have been a classroom teacher for many years now and I am fully aware of the pressure on teachers created by marking demands placed upon us by leaders, students and parents, let alone the pressure we put on ourselves. With ever new initiatives and marking strategies created by 'experts' the marking and assessment process can feel overwhelming, and it can be easy to sink. It is times like these that I draw on my experience and convictions founded on previous success. I believe that I know what works and what doesn't; I know what motivates students to improve and what doesn't; and I know that marking and assessment when stripped away can be a relatively simple device to improve student progress and performance.

What's the point in marking?

First you need to be clear about what you will be marking or assessing and why. What is the point? What are you hoping to gain? What will the students gain from your marking? Look through your scheme of work and establish what you will mark or assess during that topic. Typically at Key Stage 3 students at my school study a topic for six weeks, which equates to 12 lessons. As a minimum I would then aim to mark the student's books four times in six weeks and thus every three hours. It is important to note that I will often mark more than this, but if I know my minimum then I am sure I will be able to assess the key pieces of work I have highlighted. Once I have established my frequency, I then need to consider what I will I mark and when. My marking schedule will include the following:

- Pre-test
- Target questions × 2

- Mid-topic assessment ('milestone' assessment)
- End-of-topic assessment

Pre-test

The pre-test is for me to establish what the students may already know about the topic. This then informs my planning. If I was intending to spend three lessons teaching the students about four-figure grid references, there is little point if they are all comfortable with four figures and in fact the majority of students can already work out six-figure grid references. Depending upon the nature of the class and the test these can often be self- or peer-marked. The pre-test represents the students' First Attempt In Learning (F.A.I.L.), thus it does not matter how well they did, rather it provides me with the information I need to inform my planning so I know what gaps in skills knowledge and understanding I need to fill. The emphasis is on progress over time, not the outcome at this stage. The pre-test sets the bench mark where I can begin to measure progress from. If students have self- or peer-assessed their work I will still want to see their answers to quality control the marking. Are the answers and marks accurate? If not this may be something that I will need to address.

Based upon the pre-test students then complete their own 'progress wheel' (see Figure 12.1 for an example). Each segment refers to a key question from the topic and pre-test. Students then colour in either the score they achieved or their own judgement score based on their knowledge and understanding. The progress wheel is then stuck into their book so they can refer to it later. The aim is that towards the end of the topic the students will repeat the test and they should be able to see the progress they have made between the two assessments.

Target questions

These are differentiated questions aimed to develop the student's knowledge and understanding of a topic. Having marked a student's work, pose a specific question for the individual student to consider and then answer. This differentiated question will be based on what the student learnt in the previous lesson/lessons, or it may be a precursor to what the students are about to learn in the lesson. A target question based on a previous lesson is useful to re-engage the student with the learning. The students answer the question at the start of the lesson, which is often referred to as DIRT (Dedicated Improvement and Reflection Time). Whatever you wish to call it, it is time set aside for the

HOT DESERTS: SELF-ASSESSMENT

Learning Questions:
1. Where are the hot deserts of the world located?
2. What is the climate of the hot deserts?
3. How has the vegetation adapted to cope with the climate of hot deserts?
4. How are animals that live in the hot deserts able to survive?
5. What is desertification?
6. What are the solutions to desertification?
7. What are the opportunities to develop in hot deserts?
8. What are the challenges to development on hot deserts?

Key Skills
- Map work/atlases
- Interpreting photographs
- Numeracy: climate graph
- Sketching
- Literacy: extended writing
- Presentation skills
- PHSE: empathy with others

Progress wheel: colour in the segment related to the learning question. How confident are you with each question on a scale of 1–10?

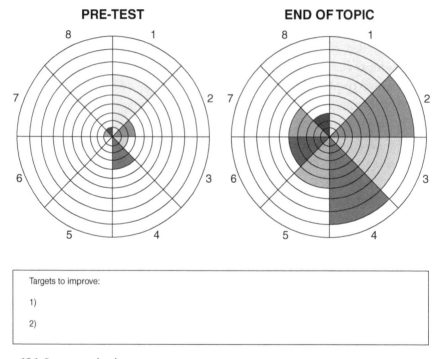

PRE-TEST   END OF TOPIC

Targets to improve:

1)

2)

Figure 12.1 Progress wheel

students to participate in their learning and engage with the marking and feed-back you have given. It helps students to reflect on previous work and reminds them of what they did during the last lesson. The question may require the students to look back in their books and reread their notes; ideally the students could recall the answer without using reference material, but looking back to remind themselves is a useful way to consolidate and apply their knowledge from previous lessons.

The target question, that is a precursor to the lesson, allows you to get a clear idea of what the students already know about the topic, and where the gaps in learning may be. Target questions are a great way for students to demonstrate or apply what they know and understand about the topic they are currently studying. They provide you with a clear indication of misconceptions or gaps in knowledge, allowing you to adapt and tailor your teaching to meet those learning needs.

Example of target questions

In the previous lesson, students had been learning about hot deserts. The questions require students to apply what they have learnt.

T1: List four adaptions of the camel to survive the hot desert climate.

T2: What are the causes of desertification?

T3: Prioritise the causes of desertification. What do you consider to be the main cause and why?

There is obvious differentiation with these three questions, all tailored to meet the needs of your students, thus students receive more personalised marking. To speed up the marking process I simply put T1, T2 or T3 in the student's book. They then write down the question before answering it. This saves me having to write the same questions out time and time again.

Once the students have been given time to answer the question, the next step is a brief class discussion. I ask questions and we discuss the answers to the questions, giving students the opportunity to amend and improve their responses. You may need to prompt students by asking them to add to their answers or correct their answer in order to improve it.

Mid-topic assessment (milestone assessment)

The mid-topic test acts as a barometer for the current skills, knowledge and understanding that the students have gained after a few weeks of teaching.

There is a school of thinking that the test that you give at this midway point should be the same as the final test. The following course of action is suggested:

1 Spend the first few lessons providing the students with a lot of the topic's content. This generally entails standing at the front of the class telling them

what they need to know, which is essentially didactic teaching. You as the teacher assume the role of the expert and you impart that knowledge primarily as a lecture whilst the students make notes and answer questions on request.

2   The students then go away and revise the knowledge you have taught them.

3   They are then tested on this even though they may not yet have the whole picture of how all the concepts link together.

4   This assessment is then marked and feedback is given to the students.

5   The teacher then knows where the gaps in learning are so he/she may address these over the coming weeks. These lessons may well be more Socratic in style, with for example more Enquiry Based Learning or investigating the questions that the students may have about the topic. The teacher then supports the students with their learning through differentiation.

6   The students then retake the test at the end of the topic and the progress is measured. If students do not meet a benchmark requirement then they go away and revise and retake the same test until they pass.

This approach may not suit your philosophy or values. I myself have had concerns over the process, yet I have seen it produce some impressive results. As with most strategies, there are advantage and disadvantages. Table 12.1 highlights the main positives and negatives of the two approaches.

Table 12.1 Approaches to teaching

Teaching style	Advantages	Disadvantages
Didactic teaching	• You can impart a lot of knowledge quickly. • Teach to a test so the students have a clear idea of the success criteria and what they need to do in order to be successful.	• Does not allow for much differentiation. • Teach to a test so there is little opportunity for the students to develop questions or to discover answers for themselves.
Socratic questioning	• Develops deeper thinking through questioning and students developing their own questions • Can be more engaging and motivational • Allows for differentiation	• Can lack clear intention and purpose • Takes time to develop students thinking

I believe a happy medium can be achieved between both styles. For example a mid-point assessment may be an extended response to a nine-mark

GCSE-style question. The question would require the students to recall previous knowledge and to apply that knowledge, yet it would not necessarily test the whole topic and thus those areas that we had not covered yet. The question would follow the format of a nine-mark question from a GCSE paper so the students regardless of their year group will start to appreciate what is necessary to gain marks at GCSE and so develop their skills. The same question could then be used in the end of topic assessment and students could easily measure their progress with the mid-point assessment acting as the F.A.I.L. and the end of topic test being the Second Attempt In Learning (S.A.I.L.).

End-of-topic assessment

The end-of-topic assessment should aim to include the relevant skills and content you have deemed necessary to master during the topic. If this has been planned effectively it will be closely linked to those skills necessary for the next stage in the students' education and also contain the key content that they will need in the future. Remember the key to planning is to keep the end in mind and therefore your assessment should be linked to the next step in the learning journey. Try to mirror the assessment style that the students will face in the future. For example for Key Stage 3 students I will design an assessment aimed at developing the skills needed for Key Stage 4 following a similar format to the examination. I will start with multiple choice questions, progress to mid-point mark questions ranging from 4 to 6 and finish with the extended response questions worth 8–12 marks.

Assessments

Having mapped when and what work you will be assessing, it is useful to follow a set procedure with the students. This clear format helps the students recognise the process of assessments so they themselves can develop the habits of good practise when it comes to their examinations.

Stage 1: success criteria

This defines what success looks like and clarifies to students what they will be judged or marked against. For the teacher it provides an explicit set of standards to look for. It helps you to be concise with your feedback, diagnosing where the problems or gaps in learning may be and therefore what can be done to remedy them. It also allows you to focus on a particular aspect of the student's work.

Prior to the assessment you may make it explicit to the students that you will be marking the work and concentrating on a specific skill or concept: for example, the use of data in an essay, case study exemplars or linked ideas.

Success criteria can be developed from the exam board, by yourself or generated through discussion with the class. Ask students what they consider the best work will include. What will the work need to include to get an A or a 9? What do they think the grade boundaries should be? Involving the students ensures that they have a better understanding of what success looks like and also because they are involved in the decision making process they 'own' the detail. This should give them a far better understanding of how to achieve the grade or score they desire.

Sharing the success criteria with students is critical to the marking process and thus improving student performance. Success criteria can be shared with the students at the start of the assessment so that they know what they are aiming for, or you may choose to share the criteria after a test so you can use it as a learning tool to demonstrate how the marks have been allocated. In either case success criteria provide the building blocks for progress as they show well-defined steps that need to be taken in order to improve and progress. Success criteria may be used to assign the students a grade score or level depending on your preference. There is much debate about the use of grades/scores on students' work. Professors Ian Black and Dylan Wiliam have suggested that the use of grades have been found to consistently demotivate low attainers and fail to challenge the high-attaining students, often making them complacent (Black and Wiliam, 1998). If you do grade or score the work it has been suggested that you keep your feedback comments to a minimum since students will concentrate on the grade rather than the comment. However, I feel that as long as you are not grading every piece of work and as long as you spend sufficient time allowing students to reflect on their grade, I think constructive feedback comments at this point provide the perfect opportunity for students to consider how they can improve their performance.

Stage 2: self-assessment

Asking the students to assess their own performance develops their awareness of success criteria and what they need to do in order to be successful. This self-reflection gives the students ownership of the marking process and fosters 'response-ability', as they become self-aware of the steps necessary in order to progress. The term 'responsibility' is derived from two terms: response and ability, or the ability to respond. I discuss this with the students, reminding them of the importance of a positive response. Do they blame the teacher, their classmates or the lack of time to revise? Or do they take responsibility and acknowledge that they could have done more to improve their performance?

The key to outstanding self-assessment is the quality of the question that students ask themselves or that you pose to them. The questions that follow this paragraph are useful for getting the students to reflect on their work. It is important to help students to develop their learning vocabulary when faced with these questions. Rather than accepting students' answers such as 'I found it hard' or 'I got stuck,' support students to look more deeply and dissect the problems: for example, 'I found it hard because I hadn't drawn my graph accurately' or 'I got stuck because I did not use the resources provided.' This self-reflection can then be used to set targets for the next time you set up a similar activity: for example, 'take time and check the points of the graph are drawn correctly' or 'use the resources provided when answering the questions.'

- On a scale of one to ten, how would you rate today's work? Why?
- Which part of your work are you most pleased with?
- Which part of the work was most challenging? Why?
- What would you do differently next time?
- What could you do to improve your performance?
- What grade/score/level would you say you are working at? Why?
- What Went Well (WWW)? Even Better If (EBI)?

Growth mindset language when marking

You can nurture a growth mindset culture in your classroom with the way you discuss the students' results and also by means of the displays you have in your classroom. Having a number of posters or a growth mindset display that can be referred to when you are providing feedback to students can be a great stimulus to change the mindset of students from being negative and fixed to a positive and growth mindset. There are many poster or display ideas that can be found on the Internet.

Stage 3: feedback

I always begin my written comments by using the student's name; I believe it makes my marking personal to him/her rather than a blanket statement to all students. I follow this up with specific praise related to the student's work in his/her exercise book or his/her progress in the classroom. This is a very important point: praise the progress, not the outcome. It is vital that you recognise the progress made by the student rather than just the final outcome. For example, Student X who scored 9 in a test may be considered 'better' than Student Y who scored 5. However, consider the progress that the students may have made. Student X in the first test scored 8 thus improving only by 1, yet Student Y may have scored 1 and thus improved by 4, therefore showing more progress. Yet who would we traditionally praise the more? I would argue Student X because he/she had the higher score and therefore must be 'better'. However, Student Y may have gone away after his/her first test and worked incredibly hard and diligently to improve by 4, thus may well have been the more committed and conscious student.

It is far more powerful to give precise praise rather than an overall general comment: 'a well labelled diagram, well done' is far better than 'good work'. 'Good work' is not descriptive enough. What was good about it? Which part was good? Those comments are too ambiguous; if you are specific in your praise, students are more likely to replicate the good aspects time and time again to improve their work and seek your appreciation once more.

Feedback talks about what students did, and discusses what the student can do next time in order to improve their performance. In order for feedback to be useful it must refer to the success criteria; in other words, 'you got this score' because 'you did that.' It is the next part that is so important and what all outstanding marking hinges on. Feedback on what the student needs to do to improve performance is what is of key importance. We must support students to unlock their future potential rather than dwell on their past performance. This feature of marking should be positive and specific; it may refer to the success criteria or it may be a specific target you want the student to work on. Either way it must be actioned by the student for progress to be made.

This part of the marking process is often the 'What Went Well' and 'Even Better If' stage or the 'medal and mission'. There are a number of acronyms used and your school may employ a specific strategy. The outcome is all the same. You praise the progress and then offer advice or a target to improve their work. Geoff Petty (2017) recognises that there are four areas that feedback should be focused on, as follows.

1   **Tasks/challenges:** feedback is given on the completion of tasks and challenges. This can be linked to the success criteria or reference made to the effort and resilience shown by the student.

164

2 **Meeting personal targets:** if students have been given previous targets or they themselves have set their own targets for improvement in negotiation with you, then you can comment on the student's progress towards those goals.

3 **Improvements:** improvements shown by the students can be commented on.

4 **Opportunities for improvements:** constructive criticism can be used to set targets for future work.

As part of the marking process I may ask the students to highlight key aspects of their work I want them to focus on. This may be based upon previous feedback I have given the students. Therefore at the start of the piece of work I may ask the students to look back at their previous targets. I then state that I want them to action the target during this lesson. For example, I may ask them to do one or more of the following:

- Highlight where you think you have met the 'mastery' criteria.
- Highlight where you have used capital letters for place names.
- Highlight where you have linked ideas.
- Highlight where you have used connectives.

Stage 4: targets

Your action targets should be based around the specific nuts and bolts of the students' work, in other words those targets that if achieved by the student would have the greatest impact upon his/her performance. It is important that the target or targets are realistic and clearly understood by the student. In my experience if your targets are short and specific they are more likely to be acted upon: for example, asking a student to rewrite his/her essay using more connectives is unlikely to inspire the student to complete the task; however, asking a student to rewrite a paragraph using five connectives from the literacy mat provides a target that is more realistic and achievable. Rather than setting a number of targets that are unlikely to be undertaken it is worth considering setting just one target. It is the accumulation of all those incremental improvements that will have a decisive improvement on student performance.

When setting targets to improve it is worth considering the language that you use with the student. The language that we use is a powerful tool for progress. Try to get your point across by using growth mindset language. Following are examples of target stems that are non-judgemental and non-threatening to a student's self-esteem and confidence. They also aim to provide the scaffold necessary for students to achieve their goals.

Target stems

- Great effort! To improve . . .
- Next time . . .
- Practice . . .
- Try this . . .
- Not yet a . . . to get a . . . try . . .
- Here are some strategies to try . . .
- Ask . . . for some advice.
- If you make . . . changes I can reassess your score.

As a teacher if you have noticed a learning need, you must build in an opportunity to revisit that challenge. Targets you set do not necessarily have to be actioned there and then in the lesson. It may be that you will not be revisiting a specific skill set for a few weeks; in which case ask students to look back in their books so that they can remind themselves of the specific target you require them to work on. I get my students to highlight where they have actioned their target so that it is clear for me to see that they have reflected on their feedback, and improved their performance.

Stage 5: spelling, punctuation and grammar

Your school may have a specific marking policy for spelling, punctuation and grammar (SPAG) and it is therefore necessary for you to follow their guidelines. For me, if students' SPAG are never corrected, then how are they ever going to improve? My focus will always be on geographical terms and I look to correct commonly misspelt words as well. As a general rule I will correct five or six spelling mistakes – enough for the student to correct without the task becoming too onerous or demoralising. I ask students to write out the correct spellings three times, and if it is a common mistake I may discuss it with the class as a whole, using one of the spelling techniques covered in Chapter 8.

Pre-prepared marking grids or feedback proformas

These can be a useful time saving device, as well as structuring your marking and self/peer assessment. Construct a marking grid that provides the students with not only the success criteria but also an opportunity to reflect on their own learning and identify ways to improve.

Use pre-prepared feedback sheets

Having a bank of targets for students to action allows you to highlight the most appropriate target on the sheet that applies to the student at that time. This can help to speed up the marking process and students receive targets specific to their learning need. Examples of generic target statements include the following:

- Practise using keywords in your written responses.
- Try using evidence to back up your statements. This will help you secure more marks in the exam.
- Create a series of flash cards to help you remember the key points on the topic.
- Try writing the question in the answer. This will help you to stay on track and structure your response. For example, 'Question: What are the effects of a volcanic eruption? Answer: The effects of a volcanic eruption are . . .'
- Try using the success criteria when you write your answers. They will help guide you to better work.
- Practise underlining the command words in questions so you are clear on what you need to do.
- Practice linking ideas together by using connectives such as: 'in addition', 'therefore', 'because' and 'also'.

Marking grids can be used with students to scaffold what they need to do to improve. Table 12.2 is an example of a marking grid for Key Stage 3 and 4 students when answering extended written responses to questions. These tend to be the nine-mark case study style questions. They are useful as they require the students to consider their ability to link their answer to the question and use case study material as examples. In addition, they highlight the importance of geographical terminology and literacy skills whilst providing the next step to progress.

How to achieve efficient marking and assessment

Our workload as teachers results in the need to become as effective and efficient with our marking and assessment as possible. Figure 12.2 highlights the

Table 12.2 Generic marking grid for extended answer questions at Key Stage 3 and 4

Extended answer marking grid

Teacher feedback:	Self-assessment: highlight what you need to do to improve your performance and set one target for yourself. Target:
	Keywords or connectives I could have used in my answer:

	Developing	Secure	Enhanced
Knowledge	Basic information	Accurate information	Accurate information linked to the content of the question
Understanding	Simple understanding	Clear understanding	Detailed understanding, supported by relevant evidence and examples
Organisation	The answer is poorly organised, few key terms are used and when used may have been used incorrectly.	The answer has some structure and organisation, use of specialist terms has been attempted but not always accurately, some detail is given.	The answer is clear and in an organised, logical sequence, containing a wide range of appropriate specialist terms used accurately.
SPAG	There are several spelling, punctuation and grammatical errors throughout the answer.	There is reasonable accuracy in spelling, punctuation and grammar, although there may still be some errors.	The answer shows almost faultless spelling, punctuation and grammar.

key points in this process. Following are several strategies that may improve your efficiency when marking, yet lose none of its effectiveness with the students.

1   Plan your marking: during the planning stage of the topic decide what pieces of work will be assessed when. What work do you deem necessary to assess? How will it be presented? Will it be an extended writing challenge or a question and answer test? Taking time to plan what work you will mark and how you will mark it can save you a lot of time.

2   Student ownership: get the students to highlight where they have met previous targets. If you are looking for particular points in an answer, get them to highlight where they are in the work. For example if I set a target for a student that they need to link their ideas together, then the student can highlight exactly where they have done this.

3   Use highlighters in your marking: develop your own key so the students understand what the colours represent. A colleague of mine uses 'green for great work' and 'pink to think' (the students need to think how they could improve on their answer).

4   Ask students to hand in their exercise book open to the page where you last marked. This saves you having to trawl through the books to find your starting point.

5   Use success criteria: ask students to colour code the success criteria and then highlight in their work where they have met it. Alternately get them to underline where they have achieved the success to meet the standards.

> **Marking for progress in a nutshell**
> - Set target questions for students to action. Differentiate these questions to add additional challenge.
> - Ensure students action targets.
> - Use pre-tests as a way of assessing what the students already know. Fill the gaps in skills knowledge and understanding and test again, then measure the progress.
> - Use growth mindset language when feeding back.

Figure 12.2 Marking for progress in a nutshell

CHAPTER 13

Homework and independent learning outside of the classroom

We are familiar with the term 'homework', and independent learning outside of the classroom is essentially the same thing. It is a term often used to describe the work that sixth formers do during their study or 'free' periods.

It stands to reason that the more time students are engaged with their learning then the better they will become. There are several conditions to this thinking, however. I could spend hours playing the piano on my own and still not improve. What would I require to improve independently? This same question and others can be asked of us as teachers when we are considering the homework that we set. Consider the following questions: does the homework serve a purpose? How is it helping the students develop? Is it differentiated? How will you offer feedback? Does it link to previous or future lessons? Is it worthwhile or is it merely an 'add on' because somebody in management tells us that we should be setting it?

For me, homework should serve one of the following three criteria:

1   It is used to practise a skill we have been working on in class.
2   It is used to apply the knowledge and understanding developed in recent lessons.
3   It is used to prepare for the next lesson or future lessons.

I believe that homework and independent study can be useful for improving students' performance. If it is well planned, developed and then effectively utilised, it can serve a real purpose in a student's education.

How to design homework and independent learning challenges

If your aim is to receive quality homework then this will hinge upon the quality of your planning. Time invested creating your challenges can prove dividend when you get back high-quality work which has obviously engaged and enthused your students. The key to high-quality homework is to deliver activities that are challenging for all, engaging and motivating. If the activities are relevant to students and they can see the worth in the work, then all this together can result in excellent work and an improving performance from the students.

Take-away homework

This idea was developed by Ross McGill (2015) and utilises the idea of a menu approach to homework in which students select off the menu the tasks or challenges they wish to complete. When I first came across the idea I was blown away by its simplicity to implement, and the quality of work it would go on to produce. It takes some work to put in place, but once incorporated into your lessons it can have a huge impact on improving student performance.

It works as follows: students pick from a menu of activities, thus providing autonomy and independence. Since the students chose the challenges, they take ownership of their learning and this increases engagement and motivation. It may be necessary to direct the students to certain tasks if there is a gap in their learning, however I will always allow the students to select at least one challenge for themselves. In my experience students enjoy looking through the menu and discussing with their partner what they are thinking of choosing, sharing ideas and considering how they will present the various challenges.

The activities have different levels of challenge to them, which allows you the opportunity to differentiate the activities for the students. The examples created by McGill use a menu template from popular food restaurants. Students then select challenges from the categories of 'mild', 'hot' and 'extra hot' with increasing levels of challenge. You may wish to develop your own categories and systems for differentiation. For example, you may set high-attaining students the challenge of completing one 'starter' and two 'mains' whilst setting low attaining students two 'starters' and one 'dessert'. You may just want the student to select two challenges from each category on the menu to complete. Another approach is to give each task a score based upon the level of challenge. Students are then instructed that they can choose any combinations of activities but they must equal an allotted score. The challenges can be set over a number of lessons or weeks, giving students the flexibility and the choice of when they work on the tasks, and they develop time management skills in the process. You may ask students to complete one challenge and then bring it to the lesson to be marked before setting another challenge. You may ask for the students to complete six challenges over the next six weeks, with two from each category. The menu gives you as the teacher a great flexibility to choose what challenges you set and these can be suited to meet the needs of individual students or groups of students.

How you design and introduce your menu is up to you. You may decide that you want different components of the menu offering different levels of challenge. Table 13.1 is an example of a menu that I use with my class. In this

Table 13.1 Takeaway homework

Starter	Main	Dessert
Create a 'word cloud' of the key terms from this topic. The more important the term, the larger it should appear in the 'cloud'.	Make a movie on the key ideas, concepts and or processes of the topic we have been studying.	Write a poem or song inspired by one or all of the aspects of the topic we have been learning about.
Write three tweets to a friend explaining what you have learnt in today's lesson or during the topic.	Create a comic strip to explain what we have been learning about during this topic.	Write a newspaper article based on any part of the topic we are studying.
Create a mind map linking the key ideas and concepts of today's lesson or the topic which we have been studying.	Design a flow chart or diagram to explain an idea, concept or process we have been learning about.	Design a word-search or crossword using the key terms of this topic.
Create a set of flash cards for the topic containing keywords and their definitions.	Design a foldable to describe and explain a key idea concept or process we have been learning about during this topic.	Write ten challenge questions for your classmates to answer based on our current topic.
Design a board game based on the topic we are studying.	Create your own learning log of the key ideas of the topic.	Make your own revision poster based on the work we have covered this topic.
Write a postcard to a friend explaining what you have learnt in today's lesson.	Create a set of pictures to summarise the topic.	Design a leaflet about what you have learnt during this topic.
Produce a piece of artwork or a 3D model to demonstrate your understanding of our current topic.	Write an exam-style question and a mark scheme based on one aspect of our current topic.	Write a progress report for yourself outlining what you are doing well and what you need to do to improve.
What do you know now that you didn't at the start of this topic? Write down six points.	Write ten multiple choice questions to test your classmates based on the topic we are studying.	Create an infographic on part or all of the topic we are studying.

instance the levels of challenge are within the three components of starter, mains and desserts. However, you may wish to have the starters as the easiest challenges, then the deserts and then the mains as the most challenging tasks. The tasks can be clearly linked to previous or future lessons.

The benefit for teachers is that the menu could be topic specific or a generic set of challenges that could be applied to a number of classes. To make it more topic specific, simply replace or introduce more challenges tailored to suit the topic you are studying or your students' needs. The advantage of the generic menu is that it reduces work load. Instead of having to continually produce a new take-away homework menu, you can use it throughout the year. Although it is a valuable learning resource, it is not my only means of setting homework. I feel that the same tasks would become stale if I used them all the time, so I use it intermittently and when I feel it fits a purpose.

The main reason I feel that take-away homework is so beneficial is because the challenges help students to recall, consolidate and apply the learning. Much of the work we deliver in lessons requires students to consolidate their learning in order to commit it to their longer term memory so they are able to recall that information for their exams. If the students are to remember what we have taught them they must transfer that knowledge or skill to their long-term memory; thus homework challenges can help to develop these skills and consolidate what students have learnt in previous lessons or during the topic.

The fact that you have devoted the time to produce such a resource emphasises the importance of homework to your students. Instead of homework being an after-thought it now becomes an integral part of the students' learning, especially if you emphasise the importance of the challenges to improve their consolidation of knowledge and ultimately exam performance. It may be necessary for students to complete a specific challenge for a future lesson. In the past I have insisted that students pick one specific challenge that results in them producing a resource that will be used in a future lesson, thus making it relevant and useful for the student. Therefore it's not a throwaway task, but something they can see as useful to their own learning and development within your subject.

The work that students deliver can often go beyond all expectations. Many times I have been impressed by what the students have produced with open-ended challenges such as 'produce a movie' or 'create a model'. I am sure that they will inspire and impress you with what they can come up with. The benefit for us as teachers is that we can often use students' work as examples of good practice or use as a learning resource in subsequent lessons.

Flipped learning

The concept of 'flipped learning' is a pedagogical approach where the typical classwork and homework elements are swapped or 'flipped'. The idea is attributed to the Harvard Professor Eric Masur and was then later developed by two science teachers, Jonathan Bergmann and Aaron Sams, who saw that rather than lecture to students during tutorials, they could coach students on what they had learnt at home. Flipped learning is concentrated on a main stimulus, which is often a short video clip or online tutorial. There are numerous educational videos that can be found online on websites such as BBC Bitesize (www.bbc.co.uk/education), Khan Academy (www.khanacademy.org) and YouTube (www.youtube.com). This content forms the foundation of the learning. Having watched the video, students can then either make notes, answer questions or conduct further research on the topic in preparation for the following lesson.

I use flipped learning with classes to develop their independence in learning. I started with sixth form as I felt they would be the most willing to engage with the idea, but I have since rolled it out to all years I teach. The results have been impressive.

I started by setting up an email group for my sixth form students; however, you could just as easily use a learning platform or shared area in the school system. I used email because I wanted the direct communication with students so they could raise any queries or ask questions since this was the first group I trialled it with. Having introduced the format to my students, I then modelled what I was after, talking them through the process and explaining how to complete each section of the flipped learning sheet that I created for this activity (see Figure 13.1). I reminded them that it was independent learning, thus any further research or reading around the subject would be most beneficial. In fact, I have learnt from this: for other flipped homework I have set, I have requested that students ask at least one further question they would like to answer created from the central stimulus. The students then have to research and find the answer to the subsequent question they have created.

Once students have watched the relevant video clip or clips they then complete a number of tasks set out on the sheet. To reduce my workload I make the sheet a generic resource so all I have to amend is the central stimuli and the keyword or words. Having completed the sheet (on paper or in an electronic version), students then bring this along to the next lesson or it may suffice that they simply email their work back.

Key points to successful flipped learning

- Regardless of which electronic format you are using make sure all students can access it. I had a lot of teething problems with my system when I first started with students not having passwords or not being able to access the work at home. I suggest that you make it possible for the student to complete a paper copy at the very least. They can then always access the video clip at school.

- Model what you are after to begin with. This gives a clear expectation of the work you are expecting to see. Discuss expectations and the barriers to meeting those expectations with the students.

- Set something that means something. This style of work should not be a simple 'add on' but should be a key part of subsequent lessons. The increased importance of the work the students will be conducting will foster an increase in motivation and engagement.

- Make sure you refer to the work during lessons. If this is to become worthwhile and truly 'flipped learning', then time will need to be spent during lessons discussing and questioning what the students have learnt and then there should be an expectation that the students then apply what they have learnt.

- Not every flipped learning session needs to be a video. You can use a range of stimuli to engage the students. I put the website address of the video clip I want the students to watch in the centre of the worksheet – however, this could just as likely be a link to a journal or a news report, or a link to the online version of the textbook. You could easily have the same sheet yet ask the students to read a section of the textbook to produce the same results. The point of flipped learning is not to get the students using technology as it is to work independently to develop their knowledge and understanding of the topic you are currently studying.

- Start slowly and start with a class you feel will meet the demands placed upon them. Don't expect great things all at once: as with most strategies and habits, you will need to develop over time, learning from your mistakes, and keep trying until you reach what you are after.

Flipped learning is essentially what outstanding teachers have been challenging students to do for a long time. Engaging and enthusing students to work independently to develop their own knowledge and understanding. Asking questions they want to find the answers to and making connections between their learning both in and out of the classroom.

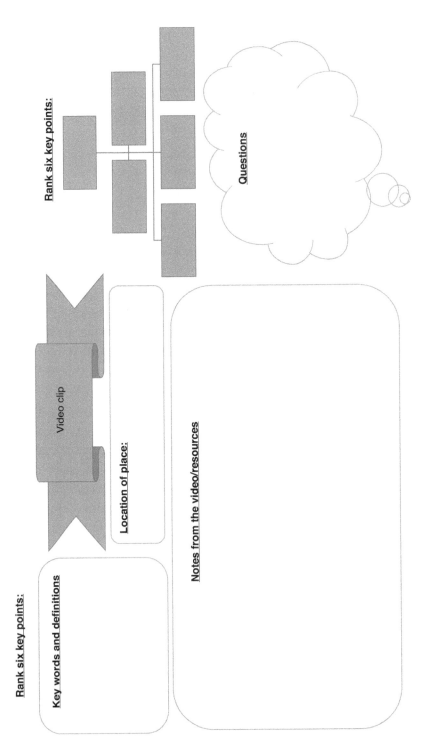

Figure 13.1 Flipped learning sheet

Homework booklets

This may be considered the opposite of flipped learning and is probably the more traditional approach to homework. Essentially, what homework booklets provide is an opportunity for students to gain more knowledge and understanding or to apply their knowledge and understanding to a series of questions or tasks. Homework booklets can also offer a range of support materials for students and can also be the foundation of revision for many students when designed well. Following is a list of ideas that you may wish to include in your homework booklet should you choose to create one.

- **Specification for the topic:** a guide sheet detailing what the student needs to know for the topic they are studying
- **Glossary or key definitions:** this may be a mix-and-match exercise or the students may need to research the key terms themselves as one of the challenges
- **Geographical skills challenges:** skills can be developed in all topics. You may choose to set challenges based on these geographical skills and include the interpretation and/or analysis of: maps, photographs, bar charts, pie charts, scattergraphs, choropleth maps, isoline maps and statistical skills
- **Exam style questions/past papers questions**
- **Support when answering exam questions:** picking out the command words, identifying the focus of the question, how to write with synopticity
- **Case study materials:** challenges to develop and apply case studies to questions
- **Processes:** challenges to develop the understanding of processes, challenging students to link ideas together by constructing flow charts or completing link tasks
- **Decision making exercises:** these challenges require students to synthesise information in order to reach a valid conclusion. These may require a certain amount of practice or introduction prior to the students completing these challenges
- **Key challenges** around the themes of cause, effect, response, solutions, the future and sustainability

Homework booklets have several benefits. Once in place, they require little management. They do not require you having to think up homework tasks lesson after lesson, and students know what to expect. They can also be a great reference for revision. However, there can also be some barriers to successfully using booklets. They are often not differentiated to meet the needs of all your students. This requires some thought so students are supported and challenged regardless of ability or attainment. How will you manage students working at different paces? Will you require all work completed by a future deadline? Do you want one or two challenges completed by next week? How will you use their homework in lessons? These are merely a few questions to consider when setting up homework booklets. As with all types of homework, they have their strengths and weaknesses. Nonetheless, it cannot be denied that whichever approach you choose to take, having students engage with the subject outside of the lesson has to be a good thing. Figure 13.2 highlights the key points of the chapter.

Homework and independent learning outside of the classroom in a nutshell

- Homework should be set to reflect, recall, consolidate, apply or inform learning.
- Planning appropriate homework challenges will increase the engagement from students.
- Offering choice of homework challenges aids student differentiation as well as providing students with independence, flexibility and autonomy.
- Use students' homework as a teaching resource, whether that be as a model of good practice or as a stand-alone resource for others to use.
- Flip the learning and use lesson time to reflect and discuss the homework.

Figure 13.2 Homework and independent learning outside of the classroom in a nutshell

CHAPTER 14

How to help students achieve in their exams

Part of being an outstanding geography teacher is providing students with the necessary skills, knowledge and understanding to be able to achieve their own goals and targets. For many students their long-term goal will be to achieve aspirational examination results, gaining success and allowing them to go on to further their education or begin a career. The challenge we face as teachers is how we can support students to achieve this. Examinations have evolved. It is not merely a case of regurgitating facts and figures: there is a deeper emphasis on the application of knowledge and understanding to far more rigorous questions. If we want students to be successful and ready to meet the rigours of examinations then we must prepare them. We are preparing 21st century learners, and modern examinations demand that they are resourceful, flexible, responsive and tenacious. Not only examinations demand these skills, but also it is what the world of work is crying out for.

It begins on day one

One trait many outstanding teachers share is total clarity on their goal. They are clear about what they want to achieve and know which steps they need to follow in order to achieve it. I would assume that, for most teachers, the primary aim is to support students to help them realise their potential and achieve aspirational targets. They know that this does not begin weeks or months before the exam but rather on the first day at the school.

Every lesson counts, therefore every lesson has to have a clear purpose. Even in the very first lesson you have with a class you should consider what it is for. What are you hoping that the students will learn? The aim of the lesson should be related to the long-term goal of enabling your students to achieve the aspirational grade or score for that student in five or seven years' time. I know that curricula can change and subject content may alter, but the foundations and skills will always remain the same: how to interpret data sets;

how to write an excellent geographical answer; how to link ideas together and how to speak, read and write like a geographer. These skills don't change, nor are they learnt in a few lessons: they are nurtured, practiced and mastered over years of instruction, feedback, reflection and dedication. Thus if you want your students to be outstanding and gain outstanding results, you must yourself think outstanding and plan for outstanding from day one.

So having discussed the importance of making every lesson count from day one, the challenge is making learning last so students remember what you have taught them and they are able to apply it years down the line when they sit their exams.

Theory: what do we know about memory?

I do not profess to be an expert in this field, nor do I attempt to shed any new light or research on the function of the brain and the creation of memories. Rather I intend to share a few pieces of research that I feel are pivotal to understanding student performance from my experience in the classroom.

- **Memory decay**: if the skills, knowledge and understanding your students have gained in a lesson are not applied, reflected on or actively used, then they will soon be forgotten. I try to apply the 24-hour rule. If the students can do something with their learning within 24 hours it will greatly enhance their retention of information. Even reading through their notes will help, yet ideally apply their learning to questions or making revision notes, flash cards or mind maps will be far more effective. 'Without immediate, then regular, review of new information, recall can drop by as much as 80% within 24 hours' (Smith, 1996).

- **Short-term memory**: short-term memory can cope with an average of seven pieces of information at one time. Thus with the law of averages some students will remember five and some nine. It depends on what you are teaching, of course, but it is worth testing this in your classroom. Give the students a list of ten points, facts or words to remember. After a set time, see how many they can recall. Ask those students who could remember more than seven what system or technique they used to remember. Then repeat the test later in the lesson or next lesson and see what they can recall. Of course the challenge is to convert short-term to long-term memory.

- **Age concentration span**: the theory suggests that the concentration span of our students is their age plus or minus 2 minutes. However the attention of students can be influenced by a variety of external and internal factors.

External factors include noise, lighting, uncomfortable seats, the tonality of the teacher's voice and the colour and design of teaching resources. Internal factors include emotions such as fear, anger, boredom, lack of motivation and fatigue. This therefore may have implications for our planning of activities. How will we 'chunk our lesson'? Although the theory suggests the students' concentration span is their age plus or minus 2 minutes, I believe this can be influenced by the variety, pace and enthusiasm that you bring to the lesson.

- **Primacy and regency effect:** put simply, this refers to the ideas that students will remember the information you provide at the start (primacy) and end (regency) of the lesson. This, connected with the age concentration span, provides a number of challenges. I find this most challenging with my low-attaining classes that require the lesson to be pacey and chunked in order to keep the students both engaged and on task. This breaking up of activities allows me to revisit key content throughout the lesson or series of lessons.

Having looked at some key theories of brain function and memory creation it is then necessary to apply this knowledge to our planning.

How to learn anything

Anything can be learnt – it's just a case of applying a few simple principles supported by practise and held together with motivation.

Principle 1: what do you want them to know or to be able to do and why?

It is essential to have clarity on this point. You must be clear yourself as to what you are trying to achieve in the lesson. Ask yourself, what do I want the student to know or to be able to do by the end of the lesson? And why is it important to teach it? As long as you are happy with your own answer to these two questions then you will have the clarity and direction of the lesson. However, if you are struggling to establish the reason why you are teaching a particular aspect of geography then you must go back and consider the importance of your lesson. How could you make it more relevant to the students? How could it be improved to meet their needs? What are you intending that the students gain from your lesson?

This is often referred to as 'deliberate practice', which includes the skills and the application of knowledge and understanding that the students practice in your lessons. If you really want to challenge your own thinking, consider which areas of knowledge and/or skills you would prioritise for the students if the exam were in a month's time. This is a useful question to fix your thinking on the most important aspects of your course. It helps you to prioritise what you teach and also focuses your teaching. It may be worth considering practising fewer more important features of the course in greater depth rather than skimming over the course superficially. I know that the balance between course content and depth of understanding is a difficult trade-off but we need to think carefully about it. I sometimes wonder when I hear teachers talking about how they haven't had time to practise past papers or give students the opportunity to apply their knowledge because they are in such haste to complete the course. This opinion seems regardless of the misconceptions or misunderstandings that may be present as there has been no opportunity to identify any gaps in the students' learning.

Principle 2: deconstruct the knowledge or skill

Break down what you want the students to learn into component parts. Creating a series of stages or steps to follow makes the whole subject or topic far more manageable for the students. For example, instead of saying 'Today we will be writing an essay on climate change' break this down to 'Today we will be dissecting an essay title on climate change so that we can produce our best essay yet.' This is instantly more specific and accessible for the students. Don't try to do too much: focus on embedding one skill at a time until it is mastered and automatic. Therefore, for the challenge described earlier, the teacher may see more benefit and mastery from the students by just focusing on understanding the command words and planning what should go into each paragraph rather than letting the students write with no direction or real understanding of the process. Share this process with the students, explain how you will be chunking the lesson and the course content, and describe the process so that they can see the whole picture and understand how it all fits together. Following this approach means that students can see progression, and they have increased confidence in the process. It also ensures that no one gets left behind.

Principle 3: consolidation

This involves the students applying their new skill or knowledge. They have to do something with what they have learnt to reduce memory decay. Remember this adage: use it or lose it! Having learnt the subject content or skill, if students do not reflect on or use it, it will often disappear from their minds. You must provide opportunities to consolidate existing understanding before exposing students to more. This consolidated understanding can then be the foundation on which to build more learning. Expose your students to new learning and then get them to practise and apply this skill or knowledge. Then through that feedback you can identify any misconceptions or offer advice on how to improve. Revisit this learning either in the next lesson or in a few lessons' time. This review of learning will inform you as to which students have committed the skill or knowledge to their long-term memory or those that still require support.

Following are a number of techniques that can be used to help students consolidate their learning.

Action: get the students moving to help them remember. Associate information with actions; for example, 'Erosion Kung Fu' was developed to help students link physical movements to physical processes. Creating silly hand gestures or movements can help students make links in their mind.

Bizarre: make your explanations and associations bizarre and outrageous, the more outrageous the better. The brain loves extremes, so creating weird and wonderful images in the students' minds can serve as a great retainer of information. For example, lining the students up to cover 10 metres can help them to remember that 10 metres is the width of some baobab trees in the savanna grassland.

Place: relate information to places or locations the students know well or can learn about. When learning about a particular place, why not use Google Maps to create visual links to the location. For example, if you are teaching the features of favelas, use the Google Maps Street View to show what they actually look like, the people who live there and the scene as if you were actually there. Take the students on a tour of the school, stopping at various points to teach part of your topic. Then recall the route back in the classroom, asking students to recite what they remember from the various locations they stopped at.

Senses: use a range of senses to engage students' thinking. Ask them to feel soil rather than read about it, smell coffee rather than imagine it. The more senses you can engage the better. Getting students to physically engage with a stimuli or artefact will prove far more memorable than simply reading about it.

Colourful: ask students to add colour to their work or highlight it to make it more memorable. When students are writing case studies encourage them to develop a key using different colours for causes, primary effects, secondary effects, responses and solutions.

Linked: link ideas together to build associations in students' minds. Ask students to create mind maps, flow charts or drawings to show links between ideas.

Sequence: sequence information in clear steps or stages to help students recall. This can be useful for geographical processes: for example, the formation of ox bow lakes, the Butlers Model and the formation of sea stacks.

Explicit: students remember the explicit well.

Principle 4: application

This is the stage where students can demonstrate what they have learnt. Once students have learnt the new content or skill, it is then time to apply it; this may be in the form of a past paper, a quiz or a short test. Whichever system you use, it is vital that students are given the opportunity to apply their new-found skill or knowledge. To improve recall, best practice is to have students apply themselves in the short, medium and long term. This can be achieved by:

- A short quiz or test at the end of the lesson based on the content they have just been learning about

- A short quiz at the start of the following lesson to test how much information the students have consolidated in the short term

- A 1-minute essay can get the students to really focus on the key elements to an essay title or extended response question to challenge students to distil their information to the main points

- Graphic organisers (such as linkage maps or flow diagrams that require the students to link their ideas) that provide students with a graphic organiser template for them to complete

- A twenty-word essay, where students are required to write a response to an essay or extended response question in just twenty words. Again this requires the students to focus on the most important aspects of the topic related to the question.

- Draw what you have learnt during today's lesson in a series of pictures and key terms.

- An exam after several weeks have passed to assess the students' long-term memory and just how well they can apply the knowledge and skill they have previously learnt

These simple approaches to application have been very successful with my exam classes over the years. The short quizzes may only be 7–10 questions requiring one-word answers or short responses, but they have helped to consolidate learning very well. It is that constant drip feeding and recall of information that helps students to ingrain the knowledge.

Principle 5: feedback and practice

Once students have had the chance to demonstrate what they have learnt, then it is imperative to give feedback on what went well and what the student needs to do to get better. Then the student must practice, revisiting each stage again as necessary. Again it is important to deconstruct the knowledge or skill: feedback such as 'revise your notes' does little to impact upon the student's learning. It is far better to say 'read through your notes and prioritise the top ten points' or 'write a fifty-word essay on today's topic.' This gives some guidance on how students can relate their notes to the several consolidation cues mentioned in Principle 3. I often stress to my students that the lesson when they sat the practise test was not the important lesson; it is the feedback lesson that is the important one. It's the lesson where they discover what they can do to improve which is crucial. Discuss the student's self-assessment as a class. Ask them 'what did you do well?' 'How did you remember that?' or 'Can we come up with a way to remember that?' These questions can create some very insightful answers that benefit the whole class.

Revision strategies

All too often I think as teachers we assume that our students may have had similar opportunities and support to what we may have experienced. I know that I myself have made these assumptions with the students I have taught. Only through dialogue and student feedback have I discovered that they have had a very different life experience or may have lacked the guidance I have received. For example I have two older sisters who both went to university: not only did they act as an inspiration to me but also I learnt from them. I learnt work ethic and also I learnt how to revise effectively. I have made the mistake in the past of assuming that the students I have taught automatically will know how to revise. This is often not the case. Through conversations with the students I have learnt that many feel that simply reading their notes constitutes as revision and that revising the night before an exam is sufficient. The outcome of this is that if we want our students to revise effectively then we must teach them how to do it.

Revision is far more than cramming everything into your mind the night before the exam. As we have learnt this will just commit the information to the short-term memory which cannot retain a lot of the information. Revision is the more the process of identifying the key concepts and ideas, then applying them to a broad range of questions and practising to improve progress. It is therefore suggested that rather than attempting to learn facts to be regurgitated in an exam it is far better to actively revise and develop understanding through exploratory questions.

When I first start talking to my class with regard to revision, I will often share the William Glasser (1988) study on what we learn. Although the study and findings have been often misused and questioned I believe the sentiment is correct. I feel it emphasises the point that revision needs to be an active process. It is not adequate or sufficient to just read the notes; students must do something with them. As Glasser recognised:

We learn

- 10% of what we read
- 20% of what we hear
- 30% of what we see
- 50% of what we see and hear
- 70% of what we discuss
- 80% of what we experience
- 95% of what we teach to others

With this in mind I then discuss the importance of active revisions and how we can achieve the 95%.

Condensing notes

For this strategy I show the students the revision notes I produced for my own exams. I stress the point that I was not academically strong; in fact my exam results were not that impressive. My success was born from hard work and resilience. I had to work hard to achieve success and it did not come easy for me. This helps the students to appreciate that I was not a 'high flyer' and that effort is essential. I also show them my geography notes so they can then see the effort I went to when I revised.

My condensing notes method can be seen in Figure 14.1, with a few additions to account for changes in technology.

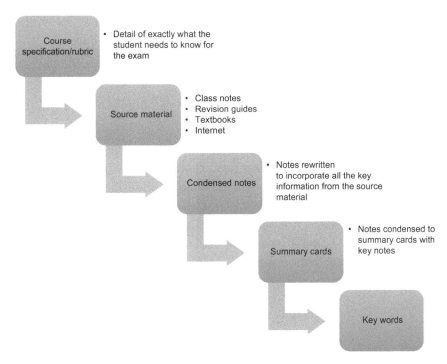

Figure 14.1 Condensing notes

The process is as follows:

1 Start with the exam specification or topic rubric. This details everything the student needs to know for the exam or test. For GCSE or A Level courses this will be the specification; provide this to the students so they are clear and they can also ask you any questions they may have over the content of the course. If it is Key Stage 3, I provide them with a topic overview sheet detailing what they will be learning and what they will need to know for the topic test/assessment.

2 Students can then use their own notes as well as any other revision materials to rewrite their notes. Students should be given access to other source materials. These may be revision guides purchased or produced by the department or textbooks that may be lent to the students. I appreciate this can be costly for both the department and the students, yet we must endeavour to provide every opportunity we can for students to access a breadth of materials to support their learning.

3 Having rewritten their notes, students can then condense the key concepts and ideas to summary or index cards. These do not need to be shop-bought

index cards; I used to use paper cut up into smaller pieces. The crux is that the students have to condense and prioritise the information.

4   Once the notes have been condensed, the aim is then to reduce these further to a series of keywords, the aim being that once remembered these keywords should then spark the mind into actively remembering the entire concept or idea related to the keyword.

If this system is followed, then the students should have a compendium of notes to revise from each topic reduced to a few keywords which will trigger the mind into remembering a wealth of information. Having produced these keywords or notes, the best thing to then do is to teach what you have learnt to another person. It is this application of knowledge that synthesises the learning. If this is not a possibility, then talking out loud about the topic is the next best thing. This process of verbalising what you have learnt is an additional layer to help the notes becoming consolidated and committed to memory.

Revision surgeries

These may be used timely when students are nearing their examinations. Surgeries will generally apply to GCSE and A Level students. The purpose of revision surgeries is to identify the issues and develop an individual programme to remedy the problems. Typically students will fall into three categories:

1   Minor: these students may have only one or two issues that you have diagnosed, which may include misinterpretation of data or lack of specific detail in case studies. These can be dealt with rapidly and the students can take ownership of the problem.

2   Moderate: this may include more specific misconceptions with some of the key ideas or concepts. These students may require more input and support to help them understand. This may involve working through questions with the student and marking past papers together to see where marks are being dropped or to clarify his/her thinking.

3   Critical: These students show a clear lack of understanding of several key concepts and ideas. They require constant reassurance and support to access exam-style questions. These students will require a tailored programme to suit their needs. This may involve slimming down the course content to the most salient points and stripping the content down to the bare minimum so the students have a fair chance to achieve.

Revision surgeries are best held on a one-to-one basis. However this does not necessarily mean that you will be required to lose your valuable time. I often conduct revision surgeries during the lesson when the students can be trusted to get on with an activity. I find these sessions work best when I ask the class to create their own revision resources after emphasising the point of how important this time is and the expectation I have of the class whilst I am speaking to individual students. I then sit at the back of the class as this acts as less of a distraction and then call upon individual students to discuss their issues or to look at completed past papers to identify those weaknesses.

When speaking to the students the same rules of assessment apply: praise the progress, use growth mindset language, diagnose the problems and set small steps to improve. Then review these steps after a fixed time period.

Past papers

I appreciate that the use of past papers is nothing new – yet do we use them to the most effect? Following are a number of ideas that may support your use of past papers with your students.

Question commands and focus: When I use past papers I get the students into the habit of highlighting not only the command word but also the focus of the question. This helps to steer the mind and keep it on track when answering the question. Thus a question such as 'Identify the causes and effects of a volcanic eruption' becomes concentrated on not only the command word of 'identify' but also the focus, which in this case is the causes and effects of an eruption.

Question in the answer: For some students it may be advisable to put the question in the answer. This can help them to frame the question and ensure they answer it correctly rather than going off on a tangent. For example if the question was 'What are the characteristics of the hot deserts?' then the student would begin with 'The characteristics of the hot deserts are . . .'

Minute a mark: I ask students to look at the number of marks allocated for each question and then to stick to the time frame of a minute a mark. Thus a six-mark question gets 6 minutes. Although this is not always the case, it is a general rule I use as it gets the students used to working under time constraints and pressure. I use the same rule when we use practise questions rather than whole papers. It can be a useful strategy to get students acclimatised to the time constraints of their final exams.

Proofreading: Once the students have completed their papers, even if there is no time remaining, you may consider asking the students to proofread their or their partner's work. This can be a useful opportunity for students to discuss their answers and also find and fix any faults they have identified. Ask the students to make any amendments in a different coloured pen or to use a pencil to offer suggestions to improve. This can be a useful and timely feedback and reflection session.

Share the mark scheme: Once you have marked the students' work share the mark scheme with them. This may be a paper copy that you provide them with or simply project the mark scheme onto the board and talk them through it. Explain how the marks are allocated and explain any relevant notes that the exam board may have provided. I then ask my students to make notes on their exam papers in green pen so they can refer to their corrections or additions later. I stress to them the importance of past papers as a revision tool. The fact is that similar questions may appear on previous papers, and thus being aware of how to answer those questions is imperative.

Depending upon your students and their confidence with mark schemes you may ask them to refer to the mark scheme to mark their own work or you may ask the students to mark one another's papers. However I will always quality assure this work. I do not assume that they have the necessary skills to always identify the right answer nor have the ability to recognise how the marks may have been allocated. This of course can develop with practise yet it is my responsibility to ensure that fair, honest and just marks are given with accuracy.

Examiners' reports: Examiners' reports can be incredibly insightful for both the teacher and the students. They give a clear picture of how students have performed to particular questions nationally, not just within your class. They provide details of common mistakes that may have been made and also clarify the examiners' expectations for particular questions. It can be useful to look at these with the students so they can learn from previous mistakes and also identify opportunities to improve their own answers and exam performance.

Find fault and fix tests

This is based on an idea by Geoff Petty (2013). The notion is that you test the students to diagnose weaknesses or misconceptions that you can then tackle to fix. For me this method hinges on the recognition that it is important to look more in depth at the questions rather than the overall mark of the students. For example, two students may have identical marks – both scoring 8 out of 10 – yet they scored on wildly different questions. Thus we cannot assume that just because they both got the same score they are equally secure on the same components of the test.

'Find fault and fix tests' is intended to be a quick and easy process to diagnose a problem and fix it. Start by setting a short ten-mark test based on key content from the course; it is best if these are short-response questions and thus do not require a large proportion of the lesson. Once the test is complete the students can mark their own work under your guidance and feedback. Students then note down the questions they got wrong and write down the correct answer. You could share model answers to questions if you wanted the paper to be more of a revision tool. Students then retake the test either next lesson or in a few lessons' time answering only those questions that they got wrong originally. The progress can then be mapped and clearly seen, and students are not having to go over material that they have previously secured to their long-term memory. Personally I would like to redo the whole test after a set period of time to ensure the material is truly secure, yet you may choose to amend or refresh this idea.

Memory techniques

The peg system

I have used this memory technique with many students across all key stages and it proves to be the one of the most successful and effective strategies I have. It is a version of Tony Buzan's linked memory system (Buzan, 2003). When you first introduce the system, it can be met with resistance and uncertainty, yet as the students work through the process they are amazed at how much information they have retained.

This technique is a link association system or a number shape system that enables students to recall ten pieces of information. Information is 'pegged' onto numbers, then that information is retained by creating a story about each number.

Stage 1: the importance of imagination

It is important to emphasise to the students that they must be open minded to the ideas you are about to discuss. Also they must try to be as imaginative as possible: the bigger, bolder and more colourful the images they create in their minds the better. Visualise the images, imagine you were there; all this creativity creates stronger associations in the brain.

Stage 2: create images for numbers one to ten

The first thing students need to do is to replace the numbers one to ten with images. You can ask 'What do you think number one looks like?' Then you work your way through to number ten, asking them what image they think the numbers could represent. For the sake of an example I create a class peg system taking suggestions from the students, and we agree on which images we prefer to use.

Following is a list of examples that students often use:

1 A pole, a man, a soldier, a pen, a paintbrush
2 Swan, duck
3 Boobs, bottom, mountain
4 Yacht, boat, table
5 Snake, hosepipe
6 Golf club, lasso
7 Bus shelter, boomerang, aeroplane
8 Snowman, fat man
9 Giraffe, flag, telephone, tadpole
10 Thin man and a fat man, knife and a plate

Stage 3: select ten pieces of information

Having created your 'pegs', now it is necessary to select the information you wish to remember. To do this I give the students a piece of text that they need to know for their exam (this is often a case study). I then ask the students to decide on the ten most important key ideas to bullet point. It is important that these points are succinct and brief. We then discuss as a class what we consider to be the top ten points, and I write these on the board.

Stage 4: making the links and creating your story

After the ten key points are selected, these are 'pegged' onto the numbers by creating an imaginative story to link the two together.

Stage 5: visualisation

Once the story is created, I ask the students to close their eyes as I retell the story. After this I question students on what each number represents. This process helps to consolidate the information for the students.

Once we, as a class, have discussed all ten points, I emphasise the importance to students of trying to recall all the points again within the next

24 hours, to help consolidate the learning. Then the next time I see the students, we start off by testing what we can remember; this is the application part of the process where students have the opportunity to apply what they have learnt.

Exemplar

The Japan tsunami 11th March 2011

1 The Japanese government sent in the military Self Defence Force in response to the disaster.
2 The tsunami wave reached 40 m in height.
3 The total cost has been estimated as $235 billion, making it the most expensive natural disaster ever.
4 Boats were washed 10 km inland.
5 Roads and bridges were destroyed.
6 Approximately 20,000 people died.
7 Tokyo's major airports were shut down.
8 Fukushima nuclear power plant suffered a partial meltdown and radiation leakage caused mass evacuation of the surrounding area.
9 The destruction of the ports affected world trade prices for commodities.
10 The destructive plates were the Pacific plate subducting below the Eurasian plate.

The imaginary story

1 Number 1 is represented by the soldiers who were sent to deal with the disaster.
2 Number 2 is represented by a swan riding the 40 m tsunami wave.
3 Number 3 is represented by a $235 billion boob job.
4 Number 4 is represented by a boat which has a number ten on its sail to symbolise the boat being washed inland by 10 km.
5 Number 5 is represented by a giant snake which is lying across a bridge as it collapses.
6 Number 6 is represented by a golf club. The golf club is smashing down the buildings that result in 20,000 people dying.
7 Number 7 represents an aeroplane, signifying the closure of Tokyo airports.

8 Number 8 represents a snowman who is glowing a luminous yellow due to the contamination of the Fukushima nuclear power plant. He is also slowly melting, representing the nuclear meltdown.

9 Number 9 represents a telephone as traders call to negotiate world trade prices as they fall.

10 Number 10 represents a knife and a plate to symbolise the plates involved in the earthquake.

Once you have gone through the story with the students, give them time to go through it again in silence in their heads as this can help to consolidate their thoughts. I realise that this technique may seem bizarre and appear as a gimmick, yet the students continue to impress me with their recall for the case studies we have applied this method to.

Roman Rooms

Roman Rooms is a memory device often used by memory champions the world over. It involves associating the information you want to learn to rooms within a home.

For me this has worked best by asking students to imagine their own home and I apply the premise that they all have a similar number of rooms. Obviously each student's circumstances are different; therefore I stress to the students that although I will be using a set number of rooms they may have to imagine rooms if they do not have them or if the layout of the home is very different.

The simple notion is that students imagine their home and they associate different rooms with different pieces of information that they are attempting to remember. However, to make this device successful they must make the associations as big, bold and bizarre as possible.

Exemplar

For this example we are attempting to learn the conditions necessary for tropical storms to form and their associated effects.

Front Door: Tropical storms form 5° north and south of the equator.

Hall: They bring thunder and heavy rainfall.

Kitchen: They form where the sea temperature is above 27°C.

Lounge: They have strong winds, with a minimum wind speed of 74 mph and maximum of 200 mph.

Stairs: They are created by unstable air rising upwards.

Bathroom: They create storm surges, and there must be a sea depth of at least 70 m.

Bedroom: Their heavy rains can result in landslides.

Imaginary story

As you walk towards your front door you notice that your house number is number 5, representing 5° north or south of the equator. The number 5 is spinning on your door. This represents the Coriolis effect that is needed for the storm to spin.

As you step into the hall you notice that your roof is leaking. This represents the heavy rain and thunder associated with the storms.

You walk into the kitchen where you notice it is very hot and steamy as steam is rising from the pans on the cooker. You look at the thermometer on the wall and it shows 27°C to symbolise the required sea temperature.

As you open the lounge door it swings open viciously as the room is full of a strong wind blowing the furniture and objects around. The swirling wind is blowing two numbers around – 74 and 200 – which represent the maximum and minimum wind speeds.

You walk up the stairs and you notice you are floating up as you are carried by the rising air.

In the bathroom you notice a very deep bath. On the side of the bath is a measurement showing 70 m. The water in the bath starts moving side to side, creating bigger and bigger waves to represent the storm surge created by the wind.

You move into the bedroom where you see that the bed is broken and is sloping downwards. This signifies the landslides created by the heavy rain.

How it works

I think you may be surprised by the results. It is the imagery and the connection between something that they know (their home) to something more abstract (information on tropical storms) that makes the bond between the information that much stronger. Once the students have learnt the system and the process then they can add on more information. The advantage with the Roman Rooms system is that there can be an almost limitless amount of information to attach. For example, in the lounge you could attach information to the TV, the sofa and the coffee table. In the kitchen you can attach information to the window sill, the pots and pans and the washing machine. This allows students to make great chains of information that can be memorised using this technique.

> **How to help students achieve in their exams in a nutshell**
>
> - Remember it begins on Day 1 and that every lesson counts.
> - Break larger content down into small chunks.
> - Help students to make connections by linking ideas.
> - Review learning to help students consolidate the information.
> - Test regularly so students can apply their learning.
> - Use assessment to review progress and set targets.

Figure 14.2 How to help students achieve in their exams in a nutshell

CHAPTER 15

Strengthening bonds
How to tie the learning together

This chapter suggests ways teachers can support students to consolidate and apply their learning. The theory behind it is that the brain learns new information by making connections between the synapses. We can recall and learn once these connections become stronger. Thus our aim as teachers is to attempt to strengthen these connections so the learning can form a bond. This is how we learn. Having spent the lesson learning and practising new skills, knowledge and understanding it is now the student's opportunity to consolidate or apply that learning. This would naturally take place towards the end of the lesson and thus this period of reflection is often called the 'plenary'. I have concerns over calling such an important part of the lesson a plenary since over the years this term has come to represent a quick round up or a throwaway activity that can be done in the last few minutes of the lesson. I believe this is an essential part of the lesson so I do not wish to attach the plenary label to it other than to call it 'strengthening bonds' or as I refer to it as 'strength and conditioning'.

The strengthening bonds session must aim to meet some or all of the following criteria:

- Link directly to the objective and the learning question.
- Give students the opportunity to demonstrate what they have learnt.
- Give students time to reflect on what they have learnt.
- Allow students time to set targets for the next lesson.
- Challenge students to the edge of their comfort zone.
- Consolidate the learning that has preceded the session.
- Give students the opportunity to apply what they have learnt.

The aim with this chapter – as with all the techniques in the book – is to provide you with ideas that you can develop and then use time and time again so they become a habit and you do not have to think about the practice. It becomes automatic for you.

Learning line

At the start of the lesson, after the students have written down the learning question, I ask them to draw a line in the exercise books 10 cm long. This represents their 'learning line'. I then ask them where on the 'learning line' they feel they are in relation to the question. The beginning of the line indicates they know nothing about the question and the end of the line represents a total grasp of the question. The students then mark where they feel their skill knowledge and understanding is on the line. Then during the strengthening session, towards the end of the lesson I ask the students to add a second mark onto the learning line where they feel they are now. It is the next question which is so important. 'What could you do that would make you put the mark at the end of the line?' This can create a fantastic discussion within the class. Often the students recognise that they need to practise more, or they feel that they need to read through their notes again. Once you have had that initial discussion, you simply say 'OK, then do it.' The students should then be given sufficient time to action their own target. You could then ask them to make another mark on the line to see if they have progressed even more.

Although this is a very basic strategy, it can very beneficial for you as the teacher. As you walk around the class you can look at the first marks students put in their books to gauge the level of prior knowledge. When you are marking the books you are able to see which students have made the most progress, which have struggled to improve and which students feel confident that they have mastered the concept, skill or content.

Word association

Students are asked to create their own word association poster. This may be in a format similar to a word cloud, but with each word linked to the next. Students may use larger words to signify their importance to the topic. In each lesson students can add to this, so at the end of a unit of work the students have a comprehensive list of linked words that are all associated with the topic. They can use this to revise from or to support recall.

I have progressed by . . .

This is a useful technique requiring the students to reflect on their own learning. You may need to set clear expectations depending on your class, for example: 'list six key points' or 'write ten lines to explain what you have learnt and how you have progressed.' This can then be followed up by asking them to write: 'What Went Well' (WWW) and 'Even Better If' (EBI). I then ask students to share their thoughts with the class; it is useful for students to hear what others have learnt as it triggers recall for them, and it is also useful for the teacher as it may highlight any misconceptions or gaps in learning that can be addressed next lesson if necessary.

One-minute essay

Students have 1 minute to write a response to the learning question or essay title you have presented to the students. This tests the student's application of knowledge. The students' work could be projected onto the board for the students to peer assess. They could then be given 1 minute more to add to or improve their essay.

Tweets, texts and emojis

These are fun ways to engage students whilst they are reviewing the lesson. Students must either write a tweet of 140 characters or less to sum up what they have learnt during the lesson or compose a text to a friend. I allow them to use text language as this increases student engagement and this challenges them to think about how they can transfer what they have learnt to another medium. Alternatively, students can summarise the lesson or piece of text they have been using by creating a series of emojis to represent what they have learnt. This is a great way to get the students to make connections and transfer information whilst consolidating what they have learnt. I have created my own templates simply by using images off the Internet of a Twitter feed and a picture of a mobile phone. Students can then either pass these around the class to read each other's comments or stick them in their exercise book for me to review. They also aid recall at the start of the next lesson by asking students to read what they put.

Picture this

Students have 2 minutes to draw a series of pictures to represent what they have learnt during the lesson. This helps students to make connections and reflect on their learning.

Key question carousel

This activity involves groups of students sharing ideas to answer a key question related to their learning. Each group is given either the same question or different questions related to the lesson. Then students discuss and share ideas to plan and write a model answer to the question. After an allotted time the students move around the room to either add to another group's answer or complete another task: for example, they could storyboard the original answer.

Example

> Challenge 1: The group plans and writes a model answer to the key question.

> Challenge 2: Students add to or improve the original response to the question.

> Challenge 3: Students read through the answer and highlight eight key points from the answer, including keywords and connectives.

> Challenge 4: Students storyboard six key points from the answer.

> Challenge 5: Students condense the answer into twenty words.

After the students have completed all the challenges and read the other groups' work they return to their original work, read through the improvement and reflect on the responses. You may want them to amend their original answer or take a photograph on their phone of the work and produce a revision resource (index cards, a poster, etc.) for their homework. Figure 15.1 summarises the key points from this chapter.

Strengthening bonds in a nutshell

- The key aim is to consolidate or apply what the students have been learning.
- You want it to serve as a book end to the lesson.
- Link the session to the learning question.
- Ask students to reflect on what they have learnt by completing 'I have progressed by …'
- Focus your session by asking yourself, 'What is the most important thing I want them to take away from this lesson?'

Figure 15.1 Strengthening bonds in a nutshell

Geography, the only option
How to promote geography within your school

The education landscape changes over time. With each government comes new initiatives and agendas aimed at improving standards and school performance. Layered within this is the functionality of geography with the school curriculum. Since I have been teaching I have seen the importance of geography grow and wane over the years, depending upon how the presiding government and schools see it fit within their framework. This then has some overarching influences that can alter the significance of geography within your school.

Regardless of how the government or schools see the purpose of geography, it is our role as geography teachers to attempt to raise the profile of the subject and to highlight the increased significance geography plays in all our lives. We can achieve this by making geography accessible for all and increasing the uptake of students at both key stages 4 and 5.

It needs to be recognised that an increase in the uptake of geography will not be achieved a week before the students make their options or pathway choices. Rather uptake will be achieved by making geography fun, interesting, accessible and challenging – a subject that the students can achieve and be successful in, not just for one lesson but for all lessons. If students have a continuous diet of the features described earlier then uptake and success are almost guaranteed.

How to increase the uptake of students at Key Stage 4 and 5

Curriculum design

The best way to get students to opt for geography is to make them enjoy the subject. This can be in part achieved by the design of your curriculum and programmes of study. Making the students part of the decision making process can help to achieve this target. If the students feel part of the process, they are more likely to 'buy in' to what you are trying to achieve. Also if they have helped to shape the topics they learn about, then they have an increased motivation to be part of the lessons.

If you have designed your programmes of study well you will have developed the students' skill, knowledge and understanding in such a way that they will be able to operate at a GCSE level prior to them beginning their actual GCSE course. If this is the case, then this can be a huge selling point. Informing the students prior to their options that they are already working at a GCSE standard will hearten the students to thinking that they will be able to cope with the rigours of the course.

Currently I operate on a two-year GCSE course. However, we actually start teaching the GCSE specification in Year 9. Therefore when the students are getting close to making their choices for Key Stage 4 I am able to tell them:

> *'You are already working at a GCSE level. The work we have been doing is from the GCSE specification you will be following. You have coped well so far and there is nothing that you will not be able to do with practise. The assessments you have completed are GCSE past paper questions and again you have achieved well in those tests. You know the level expected of you and you have been successful in the past.'*

The reassurance that the GCSE course will be accessible to them is a very powerful tool. Knowing that they have been successful on the course already will increase the likelihood of them opting for a subject they know they can achieve in.

Build your brand and sell the subject

Create your geography brand at your school. This can be achieved through the words you say, posters, displays and the publicity around geography at your school. Building a brand is a long-term goal. Unfortunately on 'options night' the usual approach can be a little uninspiring. You give out a few flyers – often the same ones you use every year – and maybe show a short presentation and talk a bit about how important geography is. This can be done well but it can often appear a little stale. However with a little forethought and planning this opportunity can be utilised to its maximum.

How to build your geography brand

1   **Determine what your students want.** Obviously, this comes with a few provisos – namely that the students are thinking of academic success rather

than just having an 'easy' lesson, and that conditions are placed upon us by the government, school and the exam board we opt to take. However, it is worth considering: what do the students want from their time with us? Also try to think like a student: what would make you opt for geography? What is it about the subject at your school that would set it apart from the others?

2   **Define your department's mission statement.** Your school will probably have its own mission statement or vision, but it is also important to establish your own within that framework. Mission and vision statements may sound rather Americanised and trite, yet I still place value on having a clear direction and outcome of your teaching practice. Your mission statement defines your purpose, and if you have a clear purpose then people will buy into that idea – both colleagues and students alike. For example, consider a statement such as:

> 'We want all students to enjoy geography. We want all students to achieve their very best by believing in their own abilities and by being challenged to reach their highest goals. For students to see mistakes and failure as part of their learning and for teachers to show them the way by consistent high-level teaching.'

This gives a clear sense of what you are trying to achieve. The statement makes it clear that you share this vision for all students, not just the academic high flyers. It demonstrates that geography is not an exclusive club, and it shows clear enthusiasm and energy for the subject and for all those involved in the department. By sharing this vision with all stakeholders – colleagues, parents and students – there becomes almost a collective responsibility to achieve the goals. Those students who opt for geography then have a clear 'buy in' to the vision.

3   **Outline the key qualities and benefits your department offers.** Be clear about the advantages that your subject and department has for the students. One of the key advantages that geography has for students is the range of transferable skills it develops through the course. Referring to higher education, it is also the reason why geography has one of the highest employability rates for graduates in the labour market. Geography helps to develop the following key skills:

○   Literacy skills through report writing, note taking and essays

○   Oracy skills with group, class and individual presentations as well as debates

○ Teamwork through fieldwork techniques

○ Problem solving developed through enquiry geography and decision making exercises.

○ Analytical skills developed with data collection, analysis and statistical testing

○ Numeracy skills, including design and testing hypotheses, graph and map construction

○ Information technology, including working with GIS and various computer applications

○ Cultural awareness and sensitivity cultivated from a world view and studying countries around the world

○ A wider appreciation for world affairs

It is this range of transferable and employable skills that I believe makes the subject so attractive for both students and employers in later life. Geography has a bit of everything, thus making it attractive to a wide variety of students.

4 **Geographical Association Geography Ambassadors is a fantastic scheme.** Geography Ambassadors are university students who will visit your school for free to raise the profile of geography by highlighting the subject's relevance and value. They can run a number of sessions tailored to suit your needs. I have invited ex-students back to my school who I know are part of the scheme, and they are able to express their own passion for the subject and enthuse the students to pursue geography.

5 **Make links with primary schools.** Local primary schools will often welcome the sharing of good practice with regards to geography, a subject that often has reduced curriculum time in primary. I have taken a group of Year 9 and 10 students into primary school to teach a geographical concept to the primary students; this was enjoyable on both sides. The Year 9–10s had to develop their own teaching resources, and the primary students enjoyed the enthusiasm and energy the students brought with their inventive and innovative teaching methods. Offering to team teach or run some geography sessions with Year 6 students will not only raise the profile of geography but also give you an opportunity to see the level of prior knowledge the students have before arriving at your school. It can provide a valuable insight into the skills, knowledge and understanding of Year 6 students. It may be the case they that know more than you had assumed.

Thus you can tailor your teaching to meet the needs of the students when they transition to your school.

6   **Make links with universities.** Often universities will run revision sessions or lectures aimed at secondary schools and sixth forms. Providing the opportunity to visit universities and geography departments will raise the aspirations of many students. It may be all they need to spur them on to achieve at a higher level. In previous years I have taken my sixth-form students to evening lectures at a local university. The change in environment and the whole ethos of a university education has often inspired the students. They see the dedication and hard work of the university students and they aspire to be like them. This can lead to them considering a degree in geography, which in turn may raise their motivation levels. Figure 16.1 highlights the key aspects of this chapter.

Geography: 'The only option' in a nutshell

- Involve the students in the curriculum design.
- Create your 'brand.'
- Take the opportunity within lessons to discuss the roles geographers have in the world of work.
- Make wider links in the community. Consider liaising with primary schools and universities, and asking outside speakers such as the Environment Agency to come into your school.

Figure 16.1 Geography: 'The only option' in a nutshell

References

AQA A Level Geography 7037. http://www.aqa.org.uk/subjects/geography/as-and-a-level/geography-7037

Bartlett, Jayne (2014) *Becoming an Outstanding Mathematics Teacher*, London: Routledge.

Barton, Geoff (2012) *Don't Call It Literacy*, London: Routledge.

Black, Paul and Wiliam, Dylan. (1998) *Inside the Black Box*, London: Kings College, GL Assessment Limited.

Buzan, Tony (2003) *Use Your Memory*, London: BBC Active.

Dweck, Carol (2012) *Mindset: How You Can Fulfil Your Potential*, London: Robinson.

Glasser, William (1988) *Choice Theory in the Classroom*, New York: Harper Perennial.

Ginnis, Paul (2002) *The Teacher's Toolkit*, Carmarthen: Crown House Publishing Ltd.

McGill, Ross (2015) *Teachers Toolkit*, London: Bloomsbury Education.

Oczkus, Lori D. (2010) *Reciprocal Teaching at Work: Powerful Strategies and Lessons for Improving Reading Comprehension*, Newark, DE: International Reading Association.

Ofqual. (2015) GCSE subject levels, conditions and requirements for geography. Retrieved from https://www.gov.uk/government/publications/gcse-9-to-1-subject-level-conditions-and-requirements-for-geography

Paul, A. M. (2013, April 15) 'What's Going On in This Picture?' *Times.com*

Petty, Geoff (2013) Find fault and fix tests. Retrieved from http://geoffpetty.com/wp-content/uploads/2013/03/Testsandquizzestofind2.doc

Petty, Geoff (2017) Effective Feedback. Retrieved from http://geoffpetty.com/for-teachers/feedback-and-questions/

Rigney, Daniel (2010) *The Matthew Effect: How Advantage Begets Further Advantage*, New York: Columbia University Press.

Roberts, Margaret (2013) *Teaching Geography*, London: Geographical Association.

Smith, Alistair (1996) *Accelerated Learning in the Classroom*, Bristol: Network Educational Press Ltd.

Zike, Dinah (2000) *Foldables: Handbook 3-D Graphic Organizers for Social Studies: Student and Teacher Support Resources*, New York: Macmillan/McGraw-Hill.

Bibliography

AQA A Level Geography 7037. www.aqa.org.uk/subjects/geography/as-and-a-level/geography-7037

Bartlett, Jayne (2014) *Becoming an Outstanding Mathematics Teacher*, London: Routledge.

Barton, Geoff (2012) *Don't Call It Literacy*, London: Routledge.

Buzan, Tony (2003) *Use Your Memory*, London: BBC Active.

Covey, Stephen (2004) *The Seven Habits of Highly Effective People*, New York: Simon & Schuster Ltd.

Dweck, Carol (2012) *Mindset: How You Can Fulfil Your Potential*, London: Robinson.

McGill, Ross (2015) *Teachers Toolkit*, London: Bloomsbury Education.

Oczkus, Lori D. (2010) *Reciprocal Teaching at Work: Powerful Strategies and Lessons for Improving Reading Comprehension*, Newark, DE, International Reading Association.

Rigney, Daniel (2010) *The Matthew Effect: How Advantage Begets Further Advantage*, New York: Columbia University Press.

Roberts, Margaret (2013a) *Geography Through Enquiry*, Sheffield: Geographical Association.

Roberts, Margaret (2013b) *Teaching Geography*, Sheffield: Geographical Association.

Smith, Alistair (1996) *Accelerated Learning in the Classroom*, Bristol: Network Educational Press Ltd.

Wiliam, Black, (1998) *Inside the Black Box*, London: Kings College, GL Assessment Limited.

Websites

www.ios7text.com
www.mikegershon.com
www.times.com
www.wordart.com

Index

Index